Thank you so much
for comming

Love

Marie- Christine Wilson

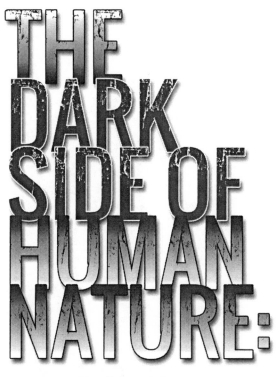

THE RWANDAN MASSACRE OF APRIL-JULY, 1994 A PERSONAL STORY

Marie-Christine Williams

Never Forget Press

The Dark Side Of Human Nature
The Rwandan Massacre Of April-July, 1994 A Personal Story
All Rights Reserved.
Copyright © 2015 Marie-Christine Williams
v1.0

Never Forget Press

ISBN: 978-0-578-15262-2

*To David Williams, Marie-Chantal and all the
other innocent family members and friends I lost in the
Rwandan massacre of April 1994. In loving memory.
And for my son Shawn Williams,
so that he will know.*

Table of Contents

1

IT SHOULDN'T HURT
TO BE A CHILD

My father, Leonard, was born in 1952 in Kigali, Rwanda, and grew up in a very religious Catholic home. His parents, that is, my paternal grandparents, and so, too, my father, were members of the Tutsi tribe. Rwanda at that time was a country that was made up primarily of two peoples, those who were from the Tutsi tribe and those who were from the Hutu tribe, the latter of which comprised the majority of the population.

In the 1400s, Tutsis living in Ethiopia invaded and conquered present-day Rwanda, which at that time was the homeland of the Hutus. The conquered Hutus and the stronger warrior Tutsis, who were distinguished by their height, lived in relative harmony in a Tutsi-dominated society for hundreds of years.

In November 1959, the Hutus rose up against the Tutsis. In the ensuing fighting, hundreds of Tutsis were killed and thousands were forced to flee to neighboring countries. The uprising lasted through 1961 and proved to be the end of Tutsi rule in Rwanda. In 1962, when Belgium, which had controlled the country since taking it from the Germans in the aftermath of World War I, withdrew its troops, Rwanda achieved independence, with the Hutu majority gaining political dominance. From 1962 through 1967, there were at least 10 attacks on the Hutus from the Tutsis, with retaliatory consequences. There was much tension between the two rival tribes, and peace, while outwardly maintained, was never assured.

My father's family was very poor and partly as a result considered him to be a burden. This state of affairs may have contributed to a cruel situation that saw my father physically and verbally abused by his parents throughout his early years. In spite or maybe because of the abuse, and the hardships of being poor, my father as a young man knew that his only escape, literally and figuratively, lay in working hard in school and getting a good education. Upon graduating from high school with a strong interest in architecture, he received a scholarship to attend the University of Bucharest in Romania. Here was an opportunity to flee both his abusive life and the political tensions in Rwanda. During his second year at university, my father met a pretty woman who was in her first year there. Her name was Lillian Dascaru. Lillian was from the city of Cluj-Napoca, located in the part of the country known as Transylvania and the second-largest city in Romania. She was brought up in a moderately religious Jewish home, and her parents and extended family were survivors of the Holocaust. Lillian's parents were loving and nurturing, but Lillian, while still in her teens, lost her father to a heart attack. Lillian had a rebellious nature and didn't always get along well with her mother, my grandmother Leontina. When she left home for college in Bucharest, she experienced the excitement of being independent and away from parental supervision. It was during that first year in Bucharest that she met my father. Both were studying to be architects, and the physical and psychological chemistry between them, along with their similar desire to escape their unhappy home lives, seemed to make their mutual attraction inevitable. In spite of Leontina's very strong objection to her involvement with a non-Jewish man (race was never an issue), Leonard 19, and Lillian, 18, had fallen completely in love.

Soon, Lillian was pregnant and gave birth to my older sister, Marie-Chantal. The year was 1977. My parents got married, and almost immediately their relationship started to become tense and break down. By the time I was born, in 1979, they were fighting and very unhappy together.

During this time, my father became disenchanted with Romania's Communist government and life under Communist rule. After receiving his degree, he declared his desire to leave Romania not only because of his distaste for Communism but because of what he felt was discrimination based on his African heritage. He was a self-described angry black man who felt the sting of racial prejudice wherever he went—in the workplace, in restaurants and in many other public venues. He claimed the whole world was against him because of the color of his skin.

He wanted to leave Romania and take our mother and us with him, but my mother, who was unhappy in the marriage, refused and told him she needed to stay to finish college. Their relationship continued to fall apart.

Around then my mother separated from my father while he was trying to decide between moving to another country in Europe and returning to Africa. In the end, he decided to go back to Rwanda and, though my mother did not return with him, they kept in touch. She wrote him often (I read some of the letters many years later), always responding to his request to join him with "I still have another year of college. Maybe next year." My father waited many years for my mother to join him. Eventually, he realized that she was not being honest and would never follow through on her promise. As he began to accept the reality that he had wasted all those years waiting, he decided to do one last thing.

He contacted some friends in Bucharest, asking them to check on my mother to see what she was "up to." Soon he received letters telling him that she had a lot of male friends and was in a relationship with one of them, a man named Mircea, whom, Chantal and I found out later, she had begun seeing when she was still living with our father. According to the letters, my mother had let it be known that she was glad that we—my father, Chantal and I—were gone. She said she had been too young to get married and have two children and that she now could "start over." The people who had known my father in Bucharest were shocked and saddened that she had made the decision to have nothing to do with the three of us, and many of them refused to be her friend or have anything to do with her from that time on. After my father received these letters, he decided to move on with his life and to return my mother's favor in kind: he cut off all contact with her. He was indeed an angry man, and when it came to my mother, his anger burned most intensely.

After the split with my father, my mother pushed away everyone who loved her, including her mother and her sisters, my aunts Gina and Gabi, changing her phone number and providing no forwarding address or other information other than to say she would be leaving the country after she got her degree. She did neither. For years, because of my mother's selfish, vindictive actions, my grandmother Leontina suffered untold pain , not knowing her daughter's whereabouts, fearful for her wellbeing and even blaming herself for her having abandoned her children and family.

My troubled mother wanted a new life, just as when she left home for college. I found out later that she sought that new life in Constanta, a lively city on the coast of the Black Sea about two-hundred fifty miles from Bucharest. There were family members in Constanta, but she felt she could create a new beginning there in spite of them. Still young and now with no children or family to be responsible for, a newly "liberated" Lillian opened a clothing store for women and began designing fashions and attending trade shows. Unfortunately, the store did not succeed, and she had to close its doors.

Looking back, I realize that my mother was psychologically and emotionally unstable. She cared little or nothing for her children or the rest of her family. Whatever her specific psychiatric issues or pathology, in abandoning my sister and me (I was two months old at the time) and leaving us in the care of our father and grandmother, respectively, so she could be free to take in European nightlife with no responsibilities, she left behind, effectively, two motherless daughters.

As a pre-teen and into my teen years, there were many times that I wondered if my mother ever had peace in her heart or if she felt remorse about pushing us away. In my most alone and frightening moments, I even wondered if she cared whether we were alive or dead.

2

MOVING TO RWANDA, WHEN OUR LIVES WERE DESTROYED FOREVER

My parents' marriage was over. And Chantal and I, the innocent victims of two adults' poor judgment, were left to pay the price.

My father took Chantal to Rwanda when she was three and left me with my grandmother, with whom I stayed, in her home in Cluj-Napoca, till I was five, at which time I was sent to live with my father and Chantal in Rwanda.

Although my father had settled into a new life in his native country, he corresponded with my mother for years. During all that time, not once did she ask how my sister and I were doing. Not once did she write to us or express any interest in our happiness. Not once did she send us so much as a postcard or a present on a holiday or our birthdays. She simply didn't care. For Chantal and me, the pain of abandonment was a sharp knife turning slowly in our hearts. We talked about our mother constantly and, though we were young, asked ourselves serious questions. Why didn't she love us? Had we done something wrong? Had we been bad children? What had happened that caused her to leave us motherless?

Leontina in effect became Chantal's and my mother, raising the two of us for those early years of our lives. She was wonderful to us and continued to be loving to Chantal after she went to Africa, calling often and sending letters and anything else Chantal needed. She was the only family member who truly loved us. Beautiful and kind, she wanted to keep me in her life and did till I was five, showering me with affection and constantly telling me how much she loved me. She never gave up on Chantal and me and tried desperately to get custody of us before we were sent to Rwanda. However, she had no legal rights and our father wouldn't hear of it in any case.

As for our mother, she completely forsook us. Even today, I ask myself what would cause a mother to abandon her children the way our mother did Chantal and me. I don't know that I will ever have an answer to that question.

When I was five, my father told my grandmother he wanted me to move to Rwanda because Chantal, who spoke only Romanian and French and not Rwandan, was always alone and had no friends. So with little warning, and over my grandmother's and my tearful objections, I was uprooted and sent to Africa, forced to say goodbye to the woman I loved and who loved me so dearly. I remember Leontina's telling me that day that she loved me and to please not forget her and to call and write if I needed anything. "I am still here for you even though you are far away," she said. "And I promise I will come and get you if you want to come back." She was crying, and it was a heartbreaking moment for both of us. I thought of her as my mother, not my grandmother. I always slept on her chest or her lap, and she would rub my hair and sing for me before I went to bed. I didn't want to leave the only mother I'd ever known, but I was given no say in the matter. Making the situation worse was the fact that I hardly knew either my sister or my father, my only contact with them having been through phone calls or my grandmother's photos. If I'd known what lay ahead, I would have summoned all the strength in my five-year-old being to stay where I was.

Sitting alone on the airplane, surrounded by strangers, I cried the entire time to Rwanda. At least I had my grandmother's promise to give me strength.

To my five-year-old eyes and ears, everything in my new country was different, almost, even, exotic: African people wearing strange clothing, living by different norms and talking in a language I could neither understand nor speak. But I could tell right away that my father, Chantal and my extended family were happy to see me, and I thought that everything was going to be all right after all. One evening I asked my father where our mother was, and he said what do you mean, where is your mother? I said I thought she was here with you. When she heard this, Chantal started crying and said, "Mom doesn't like us anymore." Chantal's words and tears made me start crying, too, and I said I wanted to go back to Romania. I realized that my grandmother's "promise" had been made to make me feel better about leaving her, and that realization made me sad for both of us.

Meanwhile, my father and mother continued to keep in touch with each other. My father kept all her letters, not because he cherished them as words from a separated or lost lover, but as evidence to prove that he was the victim who had been rejected and lied to. When my parents were together, their marriage was more about lying and cheating and treating each other like enemies than anything else. My father's decision to continue to write to my mother was a cruel game on his part to accumulate her thoughts and feelings, as though compiling a dossier detailing her "crimes." Like my mother, my father, I would find out, wasn't psychologically well, with anger seething inside from his abusive upbringing and, now, his being victimized by Lillian's "treachery." As long as he possessed her letters, in which my mother declared how much she missed him and that one day they would be together again, he would always be able to show anyone, especially Chantal and me, that he was another innocent victim in the family and that his intention all along was to be with the woman he loved but who remained beyond reach. My father was an intelligent man and had a strong need to show that whatever he did, he was of sound and stable mind, even if he wasn't. He was always right and anything that went wrong in his life was the fault of someone else. He told us repeatedly that our mother was a lying and vindictive woman. But the truth is that my father was much worse than my mother, and when the devil within him came out, my life (and Chantal's) became almost literally unlivable.

When my father moved back to Rwanda, he stayed with his family for several months in Rushashi, a city some 150 fifty miles from Kigali. He was in his mid-twenties and worried about what he was going to do with his life. He wanted to find a woman to marry, even though he was not divorced from my mother. He had no intention of wasting his time going through the paperwork involved with a divorce in another country. He was happy to lie about it, and to the very end he and my mother remained husband and wife in the eyes of the law.

Soon, things began to move forward for him. He found an excellent job as a contract engineer in construction in Kigali and was making a lot of money by Rwandan standards. He built a nice house where he, Chantal and I lived in the city. And he met a woman by the name of Valentine, whom he decided to marry even though he knew the marriage would be illegal. That didn't bother him, and when my mother found out, it didn't bother her either. She had been living as a single woman, and the status of their marriage was, to both of them, nothing more than a piece of paper, an inconvenient truth that meant nothing. In my opinion, this was insanity!

My first dinner in my new home was unlike anything I had had in Europe, and I didn't eat any of it. Soon it was time for bed, but without my grandmother there to hold me and rub my hair and sing for me, I felt scared and alone. When I asked my father if he would leave the light on for me, he said no and turned it off, no questions asked. Looking back, I see this small, mean act as a portent of his shameful role as a father and, far worse, of his future cruelty toward me.

Chantal was brave. She tried to calm me down and slept with me that night. As we lay there, I asked her about our mother, and she said maybe something bad had occurred that we didn't know about. Hearing that, I got even more frightened, worrying about what would happen to me if she got sick, or worse, if she died. Luckily for me, poor Chantal, who had already been through so much by the age of eight, was there to allay my fears. She was very mature for her age and also very smart. That night wouldn't be the last time she would help me survive.

The first six months in Kigali were very hard for me, but Chantal was there to play with me and provide some semblance of normalcy. One day our father called us into the house, saying he wanted to introduce us to his new girlfriend, Valentine Mukandirima. Before long, Valentine, who was a few years older than my father , started coming over every day until the next thing we knew she had moved in and then, a few months later she and my father announced they were getting married. Chantal and I had no reason to dislike Valentine—that would come later—we just didn't care for the idea of our father's getting married, period, because we feared that that would ruin any chance that we would ever see our mother again.

Complicating matters, we knew, was the fact that our father had "forgotten" one thing: to get divorced from our mother.

For the first few years as our stepmother, Valentine was nice and respectful to Chantal and me, even, at times, loving. We went so far as to tell Leontina that we liked her and that she was good to us. We didn't know that soon that would change, and change dramatically, for the worse.

It wasn't long before Valentine got pregnant, giving birth to her and our father's first child together. Tragically, though, the baby died a few days after being born. That was when Chantal's and my troubles began. Valentine started telling our father lies about us—for example, that we were disrespectful and didn't listen to her. The first time she said this, he hit me in the head and Chantal in the face, even though we had done nothing wrong. We knew Valentine's behavior was because she had lost the baby, but our compassion didn't help: she rejected us, making us eat our meals first because she didn't want to sit with us at the table and punishing me by making me sit in the corner with my hands up for hours, and if I protested, hitting me with a belt. I said to her, "When I grow up, I will hit you, too" and would run away crying.

Valentine told us if our own mother didn't want us, why should she, and as if to prove the point, one day on a visit to her sister, she took all the nice clothes my grandmother had bought for me and gave them to her sister's daughters, who were my age.

That day, when my father came home, he said to me, "Why do you look so dirty? Go take a shower and change your clothes." I did as my father said, but I didn't have anything to wear, so I put my dirty clothes back on. He told me to go change. I said that Valentine had taken all my clothes with her on her visit to her sister. He said there was no way his wife would do something like that and got very angry. He went to my room and looked around and saw that, yes, all my clothes were gone.

He couldn't believe it. He asked Chantal if she would give me something to wear, and when she took me to her room all her shoes were gone, too. She started crying and went to our father and told him that Valentine had taken her shoes, and that is when we told my father how she treated us and talked to us. But my father thought we were making this up, so he asked our nanny what was going on, and she told him the same thing. He then said things will have to change, but he was lying—all he wanted was our clothes back, nothing else.

When Valentine showed up at home the next day, everyone was angry with her. My father said, "Where did you take my children's belongings, and why?" Valentine said she was going to buy us new clothes, but I knew she was lying. She then told my father that her sister was very poor, that she didn't have money to buy anything for her children and that she was struggling even to feed them. My father told her that no one had asked her sister to have that many children and that it wasn't his or Valentine's job to help her, certainly not at Chantal's and my expense, and that by the time he got back from work the next day, all of our clothes had better be returned. To this, Valentine said there was no way she would take back what she had given her nieces. My father said if she didn't bring our clothes back, she shouldn't come back either. "I don't think you are good to my children, so I will find somebody else," he said. "I don't know if I can trust you after what you've done."

My father's words must have frightened Valentine because the next day she followed through on her promise and went shopping for the first time for us. When she got back, she said, "See, girls? This stuff I got for you looks better than what you had! You've got new shoes and new clothes, so go try them on."

I took one look at the clothes and immediately started crying. I didn't like anything she'd got for me, and Chantal hated her new shoes. I remember her saying to Valentine, "How come you took all my shoes and gave them to your family? That is not fair and not nice! You didn't go shopping for us for three years and now you do? It's just because you're scared of what our father will do when he gets off work. You got me one pair of ugly shoes when you took six?" She told Valentine she didn't want the shoes and gave them back. Even though I was young, I knew what I wanted and told Valentine I didn't want her clothes and that I wanted my old clothes back. Valentine was listening to us complaining about how ugly everything was, that we didn't like any of it, and then said to us, fine, keep complaining if you want, but when your father gets home you are to look happy and excited about your new belongings—or else. I looked at her and screamed in my loudest voice, "No!" There was no way I would do something like that, I said. I wanted my clothes back and my dolls, which she had also given to her nieces.

She said that if we complained when our father got home she would be sure to punish us for a long time to come. When our father finally arrived, he and Valentine immediately began arguing and yelling, and he told her to leave because he was done with her.

This was one family explosion—one of the very, very few—that had a happy ending, as he then retrieved our clothes from his sister-in-law and gave them back to us. With Valentine gone, the house was quiet, with no fighting. The peace was wonderful, but, unfortunately, was not to last.

We had a fulltime nanny, Colette, who was nice to Chantal and me and who disliked Valentine. But Colette was having an affair with our father and got pregnant. On top of that, Valentine moved back, and after an initial few tranquil days when she was good to us, she not only resumed her punishments, she also resumed her wicked practice of putting bad thoughts and lies into our father's head. Her plan worked extremely well as she got practically everything she wanted from him.

But it wasn't long before our father started hitting Valentine, too, and cheated on her even more, not even, in fact, "cheating," because, unbelievably, he was bringing women right into the house! He would order Valentine to sleep with Chantal and me, and then the next morning the woman who'd spent the night with him would leave before we got up. Of course, this ruse didn't work because we'd seen the woman coming into the house the night before. Our father must have thought we were brainless.

Despite such immoral behavior, my father was never under the influence of alcohol or drugs, which he didn't like or use. The fact is he was *worse* than people who used drugs or alcohol because he was doing everything of his own sober volition.

Valentine was mean to Chantal and me, but the truth is she was a victim, too, and not just because of my father's philandering or even abuse. He would often tell us, for example, how much he missed our mother and how much he loved her and how good their relationship was, at least in the beginning, and he would say all this in front of Valentine, adding that he would always love our mother and never love anyone that much again. Valentine would ask him why, then, had he married her. He would tell her he'd needed help with Chantal and me and then add, most hurtful of all, that, he now realized, getting married to her had been a terrible mistake.

For these reasons and more, Valentine, knowing he would believe almost anything she said, continued to turn our father against Chantal and me. Her vengeful tactics, combined with his willful ignorance, made our lives ever more miserable. There was the time, for example, the two of them demanded that Chantal and I stop calling Valentine by her first name and instead call her Mother or Mom. My father said, "I need you to show that this woman has been there for you, and I don't think it is good for you to disrespect her. So from this day on you will call her Mom. I don't want to hear you calling her Valentine anymore. She is your mother now, and Lillian, your real mother, will never be coming back. She doesn't want you, and she never wanted you. From now on, this woman is your mother."

I screamed, "No way is this woman my mother. She treats us like garbage. I will never call her Mother," and Chantal said the same. "I don't care if our mother doesn't want us, this woman is mean and bad to us," I said. I was crying, but of course my father didn't care about me or Chantal or how we felt. Chantal and I looked at each other and started crying even harder because we knew that our only chance for happiness was over and that this was going to be our new life, with endless pain in our future.

That was when we decided to write our grandmother to see if she could come for us or send us tickets to visit her. A while later she called, and we told her how unhappy we were, that we didn't want to stay with our father anymore and that we wanted her to get us out of there. We pleaded with her. She said you know that I'm an old lady, but I'll see what I can do. At that moment, our father arrived home and asked us whom we were talking to. When we told him it was Leontina, he took the phone and spoke with her for a while, telling her that we could visit but that we were not moving back with her. Afterward, he was angry at us for "telling Grandmother that story" and demanded to know why we wanted to go back to Europe. I didn't want to say and looked at Chantal, aware that she was worried that he would hit us, so we just said we missed our grandmother even though the truth was we wanted to find our mother as well as see our grandmother and, almost as important, get away from our unhappy existence. Our father looked at us and said if it's just that I will buy you tickets and let you go for a few months in the summer, but he repeated the point that we could only visit, not move back permanently.

My sister and I were happy—it was our first happy day since my father had got married to Valentine—even though our plans to leave home for good had been dashed.

It was a few months after this that Chantal's and my lives began to spin out of control: when our father began touching us. He would sneak into our room when we were asleep and do things that made Chantal and me feel dirty and shameful. I started hating myself. Our stepmother, who was still being mean to us, was pregnant again and, being constantly ill tempered, was now even worse than before. She would hit me and put her hands on me, and every time our father came home from work she would tell him a lie about how bad we were, which would end with our being sent to bed without dinner. That summer, when we were getting ready to visit our grandmother, Valentine gave birth to a healthy baby boy, and we were, to all appearances, a contented family. No one knew there was many a night that Chantal and I went to bed hungry, and worse.

3

A CHILDHOOD WITHOUT LOVE

The high point of our summer was our trip to Romania to visit our grandmother, with whom we stayed for two months in complete happiness. Because she lived alone, Leontina was able to give us her undivided attention and love, of which we could not get enough. Then summer was over, and it was time for us to start packing to return to Rwanda and our miserable lives with our father and Valentine. Maybe out of desperation that it would keep us safe forever in Romania, I decided to tell my grandmother how sometimes our father was molesting Chantal and me and how horrible I felt about myself because of what he was doing. To my shock, she said, "Are you making this story up, Christine, so that you won't have to go back to Africa?" I said no, I wasn't making it up, but she didn't believe me, which only made me feel worse. The irony was that while I had, in fact, told her the story in hopes I wouldn't have to go back to Africa, it was the absolute truth.

That week Chantal and I decided to run away, thinking that if we missed our flight we could go back to Leontina's house, she would call our father and tell him that we didn't want to return Rwanda, and he would let us stay in Romania. But that turned out to be a fantasy. Dressed in warm clothes for our expected nights outside, we ran to a park and found a place to hide. However, scared and realizing our plan wouldn't work, we decided to return to our grandmother's that very night. After we got home and things settled down, Leontina said that she was disappointed in us but that she understood our fear about returning home. "I want you to stay with me," she said, near tears, "and you know I love you. But if you stayed, your father would come for you and get you, and if he did he would never let you come back, and I would never see you again. If you return now, we'll have more chances to see each other later."

She got us new tickets and told us how sorry she was that we were going through all this and said she would help us as much as she could but that we didn't want to make our father angry, so we must go back. Then I said to her, "So you don't care that he is molesting me?"

She said, "If that is true, I will bring you back, but for now we don't have a choice. You must return to your father in Rwanda."

Wanting to know the truth, Grandma called our father, and said, "Why is it your daughters don't want to go back home? What is going on in your house? Is your wife mean to my granddaughters? What are you doing that makes these girls so scared?" She asked him many more such questions, but Chantal and I couldn't hear his answers. She said, "I want to keep Chantal and Christine here with me." From our bedroom, we could hear her crying and telling our father that this was the most confusing moment of her life. "I love these girls," she said. "Please, Leonard, I am all alone. I can keep them and look after them." Then I guess my father said no because my grandmother got mad and hung up the phone. I believe that he probably threatened her that she would never see us again if we did not return to Rwanda, and she believed that he would carry the threat out. He was very intimidating, and she was an older woman, a Holocaust survivor, a widow and confused about what was happening to us. She waited for a while, sitting in the living room by herself, crying. Then she came to our room and said she had done everything she could to convince our father to let her keep us. "He said no, so you have to go back. There is nothing I can do." For the three of us, it was probably the saddest day of our lives.

Back in Rwanda, Chantal and I resumed our unhappy lives. Our childhood was the saddest and loneliest you could imagine. I used to sit on the floor in the corner in of my bedroom and cry for hours because of how my father abused me and how he and Valentine hit me. I felt as if everyone in the house except for Chantal hated me. As a child all I heard was Christine is ugly, Christine is stupid, Christine is good for nothing. During the time my father physically, sexually and emotionally abused Chantal and me, he would say, "If you ever tell anyone about this I will kill you with my own hands." Valentine knew about the sexual abuse but never said or did anything to stop it. I hated her for that.

Every day there was always something terrible going on in my life. I cried all the time. When my father touched me I wanted to die. I hated myself and felt worthless. I would say to Chantal, "I'm better off dead than alive." She would plead with me to stop talking like that.

"When you say those things you scare me," she said. Our father constantly criticized her, too, and with her being three years older than I, abused her even more than he did me. Chantal would say, "Just stay strong. When we get older we will leave this place and he will never hurt us again." Then she would hold and hug me, and we would cry together.

Chantal and I always wondered why our father wouldn't let us live with our grandmother when he kept saying he hated us and wished we were dead. Chantal said it was because that way he could keep abusing us. Unfortunately, I could not disagree with her.

Growing up, I was treated like a prisoner. I was hardly ever permitted to have friends over. And almost the only time I was allowed to leave the house was when I was told to go outside and not come back. Even those few times I was allowed outside "to play," I was ashamed because there was always something wrong with me—scratches and bruises on my body, even broken bones. Our neighbors, George and Madeline B_____, liked me, but they would ask me why I was always so sad, and if I was the one who was screaming at night, unaware, apparently, that my father was beating me. I found out later that Madeline didn't like my father and Valentine from the moment she met them. "I thought they were bad people just seeing their faces," she said.

Madeline used to ask me why I was always barefooted. I would tell her it was because I didn't have any shoes. Or she would look at my clothes and say, this dress looks very old. One day she called me into her house and asked her daughter Alina, who was my friend, if she would mind if we went through her clothes to give me things she didn't need. Alina said she didn't mind. "Christine is my friend even if she doesn't get to play with me." Madeline asked me to take off my dress to try a new dress on, but my back was covered with bruises, so when I took off my dress she saw my wounds and burst into tears, asking if I was OK and where did I get all those scratches and bruises. I said my father beat me every day and I was sad and scared and there was nothing I could do to stop it. While I was telling her this, I looked into the mirror and said, "I'm not ugly after all."

Then Madeline said, "What do you mean you're not ugly?" I told her that that was what my father and stepmother told me all the time. Madeline looked at me and said, "You are a beautiful girl," saying she had never heard any child talk like that and kissing me on the cheek. But she forgot I was in pain, so that when she went to hug me, I resisted because she was touching the fresh wounds on my back. "Christine," she said, "I am so sorry for you. I absolutely hate your parents for what they are doing to you and Chantal." She was crying now, and so was I, and she apologized for never sending her husband to save me. She asked me if I had been the one standing in the dark alone the night before at one in the morning. "Do your parents make you stay outside at night?" When I said yes, she was in disbelief and said, "If that happens again, knock on our door. We will take you in and keep you safe. You will never sleep outside again."

I looked at Madeline and all I could say through my tears was, "Finally, someone cares about my pain." She also said I should come to her house anytime I was hungry, and Chantal, too.

I remember the time my father called me to him to ask me some questions. When I told him I didn't know the answers, he reached for his belt. I immediately knew it was time to run. "Christine," he said as I was leaving, "if you to George's house don't ever come back."

Later that night, my father knocked on George and Madeline's door, asking if I were there. When George said I was and was sleeping, he said, "Tell her she needs to come home."

But George told my father to leave his house and never come back, saying, "We despise people like you who abuse their children."

My father said, "I punish my children to correct them" and said, "So, George, you don't punish your children?"

George said, "Yes, I punish them, but I never hit them or send them to bed hungry or make them stay outside at night. I am a good father. I love my children and treat them with respect." He again told my father to go away, saying, "Christine is not returning home tonight, and she may not return tomorrow." He then told my father, as if for good measure, "All your neighbors hate you, including me, for the way you treat your children. If I ever hear you beating your daughters again, I will personally come to your house and hurt you." I heard every word of this exchange—I had been in bed but not asleep—and took safety in George's words, hoping they would spare me my father's lash, but the sad fact was that he never followed through, and the beatings and abuse continued without letup.

One day when I was 11 my father decided to shave my head because he said girls look bad with long hair. Using a dull razor and soap instead of shaving cream, he then proceeded to cut off all my hair. I started crying and begged him to stop, but he said, "You will never have long hair again." I wanted to fight, but I knew it would be useless. As he cut my hair, he also cut my skin, and blood was everywhere. Then, when he was finished, Valentine made a terrible situation worse when she "cleaned" my cuts by putting alcohol on them, causing more pain than I would have thought possible.

Later, Chantal teased me about my appearance, even about my self-consciousness about going to school, but I said to her that she would be next. Chantal said there was no way she would let our father shave her head, that she was 14 and able to stand up for herself. "I will run away and never come back," she said.

But our father had other ideas. He took Chantal outside and forced her to sit while he began giving her the same treatment he had given me. She started crying and said to him, "I hate you!"

"You and your sister are good for nothing," he said. "You are better dead than alive."

Calling my father "Leonard," Chantal said, "If you hate us that much, why, when our grandmother begged you to let us stay with her, didn't you say yes? You are destroying our lives."

I had never heard my sister talk to our father that way. I was both scared and proud.

Chantal managed to wrest herself away from our father before he could cut very much of her hair and went into the house for Valentine, whom she took outside to where our father was still standing by his "barber's chair." She proceeded to tell Valentine all the horrible things our father had done to us, everything, but Valentine said she had known all along. Chantal was incredulous. "You knew about it but didn't try to stop it? You didn't care? You are just as evil as he is." My stepmother didn't—or couldn't—respond.

Then, looking directly at our father, Chantal said with fiery determination, "You are not my father! You can kill me if you want, but I am through with this life." Everyone was shocked into silence. Chantal then said, "You will never touch me again, and if you do, you will regret it."

At first, hearing my sister's words, I was frightened; then, I became brave because I realized I wasn't alone. Chantal came to me and gave me a hug. "I love you, Christine," she said. "I am so sorry I made fun of you, and I wish I could protect you from this awful man."

One day following this confrontation, Chantal, Valentine and I had a frank discussion about our family. Chantal and I asked Valentine why she let our father abuse us. She was shamed into near silence, not answering directly, but it came out that she was angry at our father for not divorcing our mother, and in not trying to stop his abuse—and in abusing us herself—she could take out her anger on us. Chantal and I then admitted—boasted—that we looked the other way when our father beat her because we felt it was payback for the way she treated us.

More than anything, my sister and I, now that we were getting older, wanted to know why we were so hated and mistreated by our father and stepmother. Slowly, we were finding out.

In Rwanda at that time, there were no child protection agencies or laws, and parents were free to do anything they wanted to their children. That's why my father and Valentine got away with everything they did.

My father used to get angry with me and lock me in my closet. I was forced to sit there for hours, my dirty, worn-out teddy bear my only source of comfort. I talked to that little bear and hugged it, and I held my head down and closed my eyes because I was lonely, unhappy and scared of the dark. That toy was just an old, ugly stuffed animal, but it meant everything to me and somehow made my imprisonment tolerable. After hours of being locked up, my father finally would let me out. "Oh, I forgot you were in there," he would say, lying, and I would just sit there and cry and cry and be sore for weeks from the pain.

I always had bruises on my legs, hands and especially my neck because that was my father's favorite spot to torture me, using his hands to squeeze and choke. But since I was always being told I was good for nothing, I felt on some level that I deserved what I was getting, even as I constantly asked myself why I had such terrible, hateful parents. Thank God for Chantal, who, even though she was abused even more terribly than I was, would say, "Don't worry. I will find a way to get you out of here. I am three years older, and when I grew up a little, I will leave and then come back for you."

I hoped and wished that someday there might be someone to love me the way my grandmother and Chantal loved me. Then, in the next instant, I would wonder why my father wanted me dead. I would sit in the corner of my room next to my bed, quietly thinking, why me? I would cry out, "Please, God, don't let my father kill me. I will be good." That was what passed for my childhood, every single day of it. I don't remember anything good about my parents. Abandoned by my mother, I was verbally and sexually abused and beaten whenever the mood struck my father and Valentine. Some nights I would be told that I did not deserve to eat or there wasn't enough food in the house. I would walk away and go to my room, hungry and desperate. But then Chantal would refuse to eat and bring her food to my room to share with me.

There were an almost incalculable number of horrendous torments inflicted upon me during my childhood years, but one of the most hateful occurred one evening when my stepmother came home and found me outside crying, with blood on my shirt. Not only did she pass by without asking if I were all right or what had happened, she kicked me as she went into the house. As awful as that was, far, far worse came soon afterward when my father appeared and told me I wasn't done yet. He ordered me to lie on the ground. He then produced a belt with a sharp metal object attached to the end and started beating me with it without letup until my skin was peeling off my hands and arms and my flesh was a mass of blood and pulp. Even with that unspeakable torture, my father wasn't satisfied. He took the belt and hit me on my face and head, saying, "You deserve to die, you worthless piece of shit," and when he was done, he gave me a violent kick and told me to get in the house and go to bed. In my agony, I wondered if this was what it felt like to be dead.

In the few times the police came after being called by a neighbor, they would do nothing because my father would pretend to be a nice man who was only "correcting" his children's behavior; besides, the police would say if a father wanted to punish his children, that was his right. In so many ways, Rwanda was a pernicious society in those days, especially in the way it tormented its children. I was one of that evil society's most damaged victims.

Never knowing exactly what it was I was supposedly doing wrong, I lived my life in deathly fear of what was going to happen next. Some people think it's wrong to hate, but not I. I hated my father with every ounce of my being. I never hated anyone as much as I hated him, and I wasn't afraid or ashamed to tell the world. The honest truth is, I wished *he* were dead. That way, I might stop hating myself and feeling crazy and thinking I was worthless, as he was always telling me. That way, the crimes he committed against me would stop, and the hurt and pain would go away. That was my prayer.

It was only later that I was able to tell him he wasn't a human being, that he was an animal. I would ask him—taunt him, now that I look back on it—why he had had so many children if he didn't like them. Did he want more children to abuse, was that why? I knew I would get "punished" for what I was saying, but at least I had the satisfaction of telling him how I felt. He needed to know what had lain buried in my heart for so long, and after he hit me for my words, I said fine, soon I will not need you anymore.

In the midst of all the brutality and abuse, there came another time when I spoke up to my father, and as a result my life changed somewhat for the better. He was sitting in the living room, and I, with fresh cuts on my face and arms and a fractured bone in my foot, all "courtesy" of him, was in my room, as I was almost all the time, hiding to avoid being beaten even more. He had one of my brothers bring me to him, and when I arrived, he asked me why I was limping and why my face was swollen and scratched. It was if he were playing with me, pretending not to know how and by whom I had been brutalized. I didn't want to dignify his taunt with an answer although I knew that if I didn't respond he would use my "impertinence" as an excuse to "correct" my behavior. Either way I would lose. He asked me to sit in a chair and talk to him. But I refused and sat on the floor. He then started talking to me and that day, for the first time in as long as I could remember, he tried (or pretended) to be nice, or at least what passed for nice by his nonexistent standards.

He called Valentine into the room and continued to toy with me, asking her if she knew how long I had had my wounds. She said, "Since you hit her four days ago."

Not wanting to talk to him, I got up, and when he asked where I was going, I couldn't hold it in any longer and said, "Why do you abuse me and beat me? What did I ever do to you?"

Still having fun at my expense, he said, "I finally I got you to talk" and actually laughed at his own sick "joke."

"Why do you hate me?" I screamed, crying uncontrollably. "Why don't you love me? All I ever wanted was a parent who cared for me. But that isn't you. It never was. All you do is hurt me. That makes you happy, I guess." Then I said I to him that I wished I were dead because of the way I was treated and how I suffered and walked away. I never tried to harm myself though; all I wanted was for the abuse to stop.

For the rest of that week my father stayed away from me, and although he continued to physically beat and emotionally mistreat me, he never abused me sexually again.

It wasn't long before the physical and emotional abuse began again, now directly mostly at Chantal. Whenever she was my father's target, I would try to intervene in hopes of saving her from being beaten. One time, as I was trying to help her, my father hit me in the head and knocked me unconscious. When I woke up hours later, in bed, I learned that after he knocked me out, he had lain down for a nap. I guess I shouldn't have been surprised he didn't care about what he had done to me; after all, he was the one who'd hit me in the first place.

I thought of my father as a coward because he picked on people like Chantal and me who couldn't defend themselves. He also beat my half-brothers, though not as much as he did the two of us. I always wondered if this was because he was afraid they might seek revenge, if not then, then later, when they were older, and took this as another sign of his cowardice.

I was repeatedly warned by him that if I told anyone about what he was doing to Chantal and me, he would kill me and make it look like an accident. By this time—I was 11—I didn't care about what he might do; I mean it when I say that, to me, dying was better than living, so I refused to keep his abuse a secret anymore. I started telling almost anyone who would listen—neighbors, strangers, friends—about it whether he was standing there when I was telling them or not. What shocked and saddened me was that hardly anyone believed me or cared, except for a few neighbors and my grandmother, and she was too far away to help.

I didn't like to look in the mirror and hated myself because on top of their abuse, neither my father nor Valentine ever complimented me on anything. It was just the opposite, in fact.

Valentine never did anything to try to stop my father's outbursts or abuse, her way of taking out her anger toward him on us, but she was also worried for her own safety, and, besides, we weren't her birth children, or so Chantal and I rationalized.

Many nights in my room in those days, lying curled up on the floor sobbing and holding tightly to my teddy bear, I would beg for the pain to go away. But it never did, and it hasn't to this day. Often, I would run into the bathroom and scrub my hands for hours with a brush until I bled. No matter how hard I scrubbed, I never felt clean. I slept with the lights on because I was afraid of the dark and fearful that a dark room would make it easier for my father to abuse me. All I wanted was to be free, to be away from this animal who cast a shadow of darkness and evil that would end up lasting a lifetime.

As I have said, Valentine suffered from my father's brutality, too. For example, often, at dinner, he would erupt and tell her how much he hated her and ask rhetorically why he had ever married her. Then, for no reason, he would hit her, and though she would beg him to stop, he would keep on hitting her, saying, "You make my life miserable." It was as if he were the victim, not us. This was part of his sickness.

He would use any pretense to beat us. One time I came home with a report card he didn't like, so he kicked me until I became unconscious. I called our house the devil's house. Not once did I hear my father say good morning or good afternoon or offer praise for a job well done. To him, everything everyone did was wrong. Was this another symptom of his sickness? There was no doubt in my mind.

I repeatedly begged him to let Chantal and me go back to Europe, but he would always refuse. I guess he wanted us at his devil's house to be slaves he could abuse at will. If so, he deserved a trophy, with his children and Valentine emblazoned on the sides. The abuse we suffered was such that for many years Chantal and I grew up thinking it was normal to be beaten and hated by your parents.

Sometimes, when I was particularly miserable—or brave, or maybe foolhardy—I would leave the house and run for hours. The only person who worried, let alone cared, about me during those long absences was Chantal. When I returned, she would hug me and ask if I was all right while my father would threaten me with a beating. One time, feeling brave or rash, not being able to stand another day in that house and remembering when Chantal and I had run away to keep from being sent back to Rwanda, I decided to leave, I thought, for good. I was 11 at the time. I packed my things, which amounted to a pathetically small amount of very old clothes and toys, and left the house without anyone's knowing. After a few hours, it started to rain, so I decided, reluctantly, to go back, and as I walked through the door, my father saw me and asked where I had been. As usual with his interrogations, I was too frightened to answer, so, also as usual, he beat me. I then realized that if I wanted to rid myself of this devil, I would have to leave and never return.

There was no other way to describe it: my life was full of lies and sadness. Every Christmas we had a tree with presents, and it was always the same: "Sorry, Christine. We didn't have enough money to buy you anything. Maybe next year." Looking back, I would say that was a perfect metaphor for my life in those days: nothing but disappointment and unhappiness.

In my house, you weren't allowed to ask questions. Whenever Chantal or I asked my father something he would say how dare you, and almost always drive the point home with a beating. The only question I asked was of myself or Chantal: Was a different life possible?

One night, Valentine said she "kind of knew" that our father had been molesting Chantal and me (and that he had lied about divorcing our mother). She claimed she had begged him to stop touching us but got beaten for her effort. She said our father denied our accusations and insisted we were lying. Then she pointed out to Chantal and me that she, too, was mistreated by him. I looked at her and said, "Stop playing the victim. You are the one who started this with your lies about us. Before you came, he was a good father."

Later that night, my father blamed our mother for the family's problems, saying, "She didn't want to take care of you, so she dumped you on me, and I didn't want you, either." I could never, ever imagine saying such terrible, hurtful things about one's children, but my father obviously had no qualms. Then he told us how our mother had been "cheating" on him and that he wondered whether Chantal and I were actually his daughters or someone else's. Hearing this, Chantal said, "I'm glad you told me that because as much as I hate you, I feel you aren't my father, either."

That was all our father needed to hear. He grabbed Chantal by the neck and pushed her against a wall. I got a mop and started hitting him, yelling for him to stop. I kept hitting him until he finally let her go. But then he grabbed me and said, "Don't you *dare* talk to me like that!" and hit me with the mop over and over. Still, I was happy I could rescue Chantal and only too glad to trade my beating for hers.

By my early teens, I was very strong and took it upon myself to protect Chantal whenever possible. But because of the unrelenting stress at home, my schoolwork had started to suffer, and my teachers began to worry about me. Their worries, though, went only so far, as African teachers, sharing the values of the community, were abusive to their students and wouldn't hesitate to use corporal punishment when "deserved"—or when not.

Classrooms were divided into two sections: on one side were the Hutu children, on the other the Tutsi children. Teachers used sticks to maintain "order," with the Hutu teachers hitting and verbally abusing the Tutsi children, and the Tutsi teachers doing the same to the Hutu children. I had a Hutu teacher and so was beaten often.

I had five half-brothers, all younger than I—Adrian, 9; Placide, 8; Shadrac, 6; Fabrice, 5; and William, 2. They were all rambunctious, and every time they caused a problem, they would blame it on me and therefore, because Valentine was there to protect them, usually escape punishment.

One morning I woke up determined to defend myself (and Chantal,) regardless of the cost to my safety. I decided that if my father or Valentine hit me, I would hit them back, especially my father. Later that day, during an argument, my father repeated what he had said before about our mother, only with a twist. "I never wanted to have you," he said. "It was your mother's fault; she was supposed to abort you, but it was illegal and you could go to jail for a long time. That's the only reason you're around today." That was the day I said to my father, "If you ever hit me again, I will pay you back, and if your kids lie about me, I will hit them, and if Valentine starts fighting with me, she will never forget that this time I will protect myself."

As a result of my life of abuse and debasement, I became violent and mean even as I somehow hoped this would help me get what I wanted most: the love of my parents. More than anything, I yearned for someone to hold me when I was frightened or when I had a bad dream, someone to love me and protect me when I was hurt. For as long as I could remember in that miserable house, that had been my dream. But it was never to be. Ever. The only "loved one" I could count on other than Chantal was my tattered, dirty, beaten-up teddy bear, which I never even got around to naming, my sole meaningful possession, my escape, my hope, my support. One black day, my father, in one of his most twisted acts, grabbed the teddy bear from me when I was reeling from his abuse and threw it into a charcoal fire for a cookout. My teddy bear was being destroyed in a fire! I couldn't believe it. Chantal, who loved me so much, watched this and suffered almost as much as I did. As it turned out, my father's unforgivable act was one of the moments in my life that changed everything.

4

THE SADNESS AND ANGER OF AN ABUSED CHILD

My father, feeling smug and satisfied with himself as though he hadn't a care in the world, finished his lunch and was sleeping in his favorite chair. Chantal was in her room. Valentine was talking to the neighbors, and my brothers were outside playing with their friends. And I, in my room mourning the loss of my teddy bear and contemplating my response, decided I'd had enough. I told myself now was the time to respond to my father for all the abuse and pain, to gain revenge and to keep myself safe from further attacks. I went to the grill where my teddy bear had been destroyed and found a teapot of boiling water, a large African teapot that held a lot of water for our big family. I grabbed the teapot and walked over to where my father was sleeping contentedly in his chair. It was all in front of me. I wanted him to stop hitting and molesting me. I was beyond desperate to put an end to the misery and determined to carry out my plan no matter what. I knew an act of violence was the only thing this awful man would understand. He had molested me the night before and now my teddy bear, my friend and confidante, was in ashes. So I took the teapot and dumped that boiling water on his legs and screamed, "Leonard, you will never hit me, you will never yell at me, you will never molest me again. I will no longer

THE DARK SIDE OF HUMAN NATURE

be your slave, and the next time you touch me I will burn your face, and I won't care if I go to jail for the rest of my life!"

He leaped up yelling. "She just burned me!" He shouted to Valentine for help while I calmly walked away and said, "Believe me. I will burn your face next time. I am not joking."

He was shrieking in pain and running toward the shower, saying, "Christine, I will kill you! I can't believe you just burned my legs!" Chantal heard everything but had learned long ago to ignore the daily screaming in the house. For their part, Valentine and her sons, who were still outside, didn't hear or see any of the confrontation.

My father couldn't fathom what I had done. And, to be honest, neither could I, because even though I despised him, even though I had threatened him before and even though I thought he deserved it, I never really wanted to hurt him. My act was more a sign of my desperation than of vindictiveness—not that I wouldn't have been entitled to an act of vindictiveness, one even worse than the one I carried out, after what he'd put me through.

While he was in the shower trying to get relief, I was in my room packing in case he ordered me to leave the house. I put my bags in the guest house and then went to the back yard and sat on the ground, not knowing what to do or what would happen to me. The only thing I knew for sure was that I didn't regret what I had done.

When I told Chantal about the "burning," she was in disbelief and frightened for me. Putting on a brave front, I told her I wasn't worried. Shortly afterward, Valentine, having learned about what had happened, became very angry and threatening, but I stood up to her, drawing strength from my belief that she might think I would do the same thing to her.

A little while later, Colette returned from grocery shopping and was told about the incident. She started laughing. "You really burned him?" she said, incredulously. "You finally defended yourself, Christine! I am proud of you and glad you did what you did because that man deserved it."

Then, turning to Valentine, she said she was sick of witnessing the abuse and mistreatment of Chantal and me. "You refuse to even buy a pair of shoes for Christine or buy her a birthday present, but you have the money to pay me every month?" she said. By now, her laughter had nearly turned to tears.

Valentine said, "You are on her side now?"

"I have been on her side since the first day I saw her," Agnes said. "She is my friend and I love her. To be honest, she is the only reason I've stayed here. I didn't want to abandon this beautiful child to you and your dog of a husband."

Soon my father appeared and the moment of truth was at hand. Enraged and pointing to his scalded legs, he told me I was grounded for a week and that "you will not eat my food, either." Then he said he was going to the hospital because of what I had done, as if he were expecting my sympathy or trying to make me feel guilty.

I'd somehow intuitively discovered that bullies, most of the time, are nothing more than cowards—sometimes sick and warped cowards, but cowards just the same—and that they will back down when confronted by someone who stands up to them. Looking at my father at that moment, I realized the coward that I saw in him was, if not afraid, then at least wary of me. He realized that I was a growing girl and no longer the passive "slave" he could abuse without fear of retribution. I now posed a physical threat to him. More ominously by far, I think he now realized that I might actually kill him before he killed me. Calling him by his first name again (something strictly forbidden in African culture), I said, "You have a choice. Leave me alone or there will be a war between us, a war that I guarantee you I will win."

He went to the hospital where he was given ointment to put on his wounds and told he would have permanent scars on his legs. When, trying to make me feel bad, he told me that, I said that I had scars caused by him, so we were even. Then he had the gall to say I owed him an apology. I told him he'd never apologized to me for a lifetime of abuse, that he was an animal and that he would never get an apology from me. The minute the words were out of my mouth, I knew what was coming. He started walking toward me, and before I could get away, grabbed me by my neck, pushed me against a wall and kicked me as hard as he could in my stomach." I am your father, and when I ask you to do something you do it!"

"No, Leonard, you are not my father," I said, heaving and screaming. "I don't have a father and never will have one!"

He repeated his sick fantasy that he was only trying to "teach and correct" me, which made me cry even more. I repeated my denunciation of him as an animal and someone I hated as much as it was possible to hate and my warning that if he ever abused me again I would kill him. At that point, he chose to remind me that he was the "boss" in his house and if I didn't like his "rules," I could leave. As I had already packed my bags in expectation of just such an ultimatum, I said to him, "I will never forget how many times I was punished for something I didn't do or sent to bed without eating or sent to school without lunch or money to buy food or told how stupid I was." With that, and not wanting to hear more of his lies, I ran to the guest house, got my bags and left to stay with family friends, giving him what he claimed he wanted: my absence from his house. I stayed away from the house, that devil's house, for an entire week, a long time for a young teenage girl.

Around this time, it came to be that Colette had gotten pregnant by our father, and when Valentine learned of it, she threw her out of the house. Upon discovering this, my father physically attacked Valentine, hitting her and throwing her down and telling her if she didn't like it she could take her children and leave. Then, after the baby was born, Colette came back to the house to show the infant to my father and to ask for money, proudly and happily announcing to Chantal and me that we had a new baby sister, Alice. When my father got home, he told Colette that he was keeping the baby and gave her five hundred Rwandan francs—the equivalent of one U.S. dollar.

When I was 12, and with no indication to anyone as to what was coming, my father decided to change his life and began attending a Pentecostal church near our home. He started praying every day and engaging in fasting to proclaim the presence of God in his life. More astonishingly, and more brazenly, he asked Chantal and me to forgive him for what he had done to us. I told him my forgiveness would come only when I was dead and that he was asking for it now because he'd come to be afraid of me. "I don't trust you or your religion," I said. "Leave me alone."

He subsequently asked me many times to forgive him, and I always said no, that it was too late. I told him if he really wanted to make up for destroying my life he should let me grieve in peace. From then on, I hid from him. If it was a weekend and he was at home, I would stay in my room. At lunch time, I would take my food from the kitchen to my room before he could see me. I would stay locked in my room and ignore his knock at my door. I would not talk to him. All I wanted was peace. It seemed to work: for the first time in my long, unhappy life, he respected my wishes and left me alone.

I would hear him in the morning praying, and the first thing that came to my mind was "You must be kidding; I can't believe you are praying!" There is no way God will hear your prayers, I said; you are wasting your time. There he was, going to church on a regular basis, saying a blessing for his food and reading his Bible, but to me it was all because Chantal and I were growing, and he was worried that he could no longer abuse us without fear of payback, or that his awful secret would get out. Why, if he was "changing," and even though he had stopped abusing Chantal and me sexually, did he continue to beat us?

Then Valentine began going to church with him, and suddenly the family started calling itself Christian. I was in disbelief. But, as my father had seemed to transform himself into something new and was trying to treat us better, I started to think that maybe even terrible people could change and that I was witnessing a miracle of sorts. I began to feel that if I started going to church, maybe God would give me peace, that if he could change bad people like my father, maybe he could heal my shattered life.

I wanted this to be my own decision, not one forced on me by my family, to follow my heart and choose my own church, especially since the last thing I wanted was to go to the same church my father was attending. All I desired was peace and to believe in and trust God, even though he hadn't answered my prayers as a child when I needed him.

By now my father had become obsessed with church and was forcing us to pray as a family every night and get up at 5 in the morning to sing church songs. I began to believe more and more that he had changed, and as he continued to get more religious, felt my doubts about the sincerity of his "conversion" melt away although I wasn't ready to trust him completely. Besides, he was still hitting Chantal and me and Valentine. Almost before I knew it, though, the whole family started getting involved in church, Sunday school and Bible study, and we established a more-or-less normal family life. Even the beatings, while still occurring, weren't as bad as before. And there was the fact that Chantal and I were no longer being touched sexually.

One morning I was talking to Chantal, who was feeling sad and teary eyed. When I asked her what was wrong, she turned away and didn't answer. I immediately feared the worst and told her it was OK if she didn't want to talk about it. I also told her I thought I knew what was hurting her. Wiping her tears, she looked at me and said, "How did you know?" It was then that I told her for the first time that our father had been molesting me my whole life. One reason we hadn't known about each other was that he had forced us to sleep in separate bedrooms in spite of our pleas to sleep together. This was his sick ploy to keep molesting us in secret.

Chantal then told me everything: her memories, her nightmares, how she felt worthless and dirty, how she wished she had never been born, how her horrible past was following her everywhere and how she feared he would do it again. It sounded all-too-sickeningly familiar.

I held her and told her I loved her and that someday we would leave that house forever and start a new life somewhere else. I said the reason I never told her about what our father had done to me was that I had never thought that he was also doing it to her. Afterward, as we grew older and shared the awful details of our abuse, we became closer than ever and pledged to protect each other from the monster that was this man.

We decided that Valentine needed to know about what our father had done, so we brought her into Chantal's room at this time and told her everything, including my reasons for having burned him. As we talked, Chantal and I cried and hugged each other and made a pact that no matter what happened, we would do anything and everything to stop our father from ever hurting us again. Upon hearing our story, Valentine sat motionless. Eventually, she said she was sorry about what had happened but that there was nothing she could do. Chantal and I were shocked at her heartlessness. "You're the only mother we've known, and all you can say is a worthless 'I'm sorry'"?

She then told us, "Your father treats me almost as badly he treats you. He even forced our nanny to have sex with him and has slept with every nanny we've ever had." We couldn't believe what she'd just said. Chantal jumped up and asked her to repeat it. Our father had raped his sister-in-law? Chantal stated that he was clearly insane, that something was wrong in his head. It just confirmed for us that he was a child of the devil, that he was hated by everyone, that no one ever had anything good to say about him and that once people got to know him they would flee and want to have nothing to do with him. Valentine continued to open up to us, even taking off her shirt to show how her back was covered with welts. With tears in her eyes, she said, "My children, your father hits me with a belt every night, and I don't know what to do. I can't take it anymore, but I am nine years older than he is and maybe he treats me like this because of my age." She asked us, "How can I be expected to protect you if I can't protect myself?" Chantal said we should call the police and tell them what was going on. But Valentine reminded us that in Rwanda there were no laws against spousal and child abuse, so we had no choice but to keep the cruelty to ourselves. "If your father were even to find out that we've been talking about this among ourselves, he would have his retribution."

I said, "If he touches me or either you, I will fight him, I am tired of all this years of abuse. I will stand up for myself just like I did before, only this time I will burn his face off!" Valentine then apologized from her heart to Chantal and me for having mistreated us and told us it would never happen again. She told us that, appallingly, our father once told her that if she were nice to us, we would never listen to her. She apologized again and said she loved us. It was the first time we'd ever heard her say that.

Our father continued to force us to go to church and pray with him, but Chantal, Valentine and I were never comfortable doing this because we still doubted that his "conversion" was anything other than a pretense to mask his crimes (I call them crimes; even though no one punished him , they were crimes in the eyes of the civilized world and certainly were crimes to me) and to show that he was a normal person. To our surprise and despite our initial misgivings about the spiritual life, my sister and I found ourselves loving the church-going experience, especially singing in the choir with our new friends and spending time with other Christian children. We were now seeing life from a different point of view.

Whether our father's conversion was real or counterfeit, the fact was that our family was trying to change their behavior, and you could see the changes. But they had a long way to go. I still had nightmares, and for my entire childhood I was scared to go to bed, scared of the dark, scared even of being hiding under my covers. All I had known was pain, punishment, degradation and abuse. I never heard anyone in my family say anything good; everybody was angry and unhappy all the time. My father would ask me if I had any homework, and if I said yes, he would give me ten minutes to finish it. I would tell him I had twenty pages and it was not possible to finish it in ten minutes; he would say I don't care, it's not my problem. After ten minutes, he would ask if I had finished my work. When I told him no, he would take out his belt and start beating me with the buckle. Then he would pull my ears and pinch me hard in the face. I would grab my homework and run to my room where I would hide and cry and lock myself up the rest of the day or night. As horrific as that was, it was nothing compared to the terrible other things he did to me, at night in my room.

My father never missed an opportunity to belittle people. For example, he would get a chair and go out in the back yard were everyone was sitting and take out pictures of our mother and tell nice stories about her. Then he would throw a picture to Valentine and say, "You will never be like her. She was a beautiful women," telling her that she was fat and good for nothing.

Valentine would be hurt and angry and later, after sending her children outside to play, would order me to clean up after them—to clean their rooms and wash their dishes—using me to vent her rage at my father.

If there was "peace" in our house it was peace by our family's miserable standards. For example, there was the time Yves and Nicole Kagina came over for dinner. They were a nice couple who lived in another city. Looking around, Mr. Kagina asked why it was that everyone was at the table except Chantal and me. My father said, "I don't know. They're around here somewhere," which of course was a lie. Then he summoned us to the dining room, but his ploy backfired when Mr. Kagina asked Chantal why we weren't eating with everyone else.

"Our father said we couldn't because we were punished," she said.

Then I said, "It's OK if they don't want us to eat their food. I'm almost fifteen, and I don't care anymore how they treat us."

Then Mrs. Kagina, who with her husband had been planning to spend the night, got up and said, "I wish I had known this before coming here. Christine, Chantal, I am so sorry." She became visibly upset. "If you need anything, please call me, and I will come for you." She looked at my father and said, "I forced Yves to come with me tonight; he doesn't even like you, but he's here because he loves me."

For one of the few times in his life, my father actually seemed ashamed. He apologized to the Kaginas and implored them to stay, but his appeal went nowhere; they were already on their way out, again telling Chantal and me they were sorry for our terrible circumstances and repeating their invitation to call them if we needed help.

Afterward, I could tell my father wanted to hit me for my "impudence." But now that I was older, the beatings had stopped. I said, "I feel sorry for you, Leonard. You just lost your friends." Then I said, "I'm not going to lie to protect you and I'm not scared of you anymore." I made sure to call him by his first name because I knew that

that made him mad, as he thought it was the height of insolence for a child, and a female child at that, to be so familiar. To myself, I called him by the nickname I had given him, Mijyojyo, Rwandan for "contentious, angry man."

As a fourteen-year-old, I became more confident and protective of my sister and myself. I not only called my father by his first name but told him to call me Chris, a name I preferred because in those days I dressed and carried myself like a boy. I stood up to him and to Valentine, especially when they—mainly my father—would demand to see Chantal "to discuss something." I would tell him I was be the go-between for her, and seeing my determination, he would give up and walk away.

By now, Valentine was apologizing to Chantal and me all the time, but I reminded her that she had helped destroy our lives. Nevertheless, because she too had suffered, I told her I forgave her but also made sure she knew I wouldn't or couldn't forget.

If my father's and Valentine's beatings stopped, their hurtful treatment continued. When I turned 14, there was no party, no presents, no hugs, barely even a mention of the occasion. Thanks to them, my bad dreams never stopped, and I was beginning to wonder if I would ever have a comforting night's sleep ones in my life.

Chantal, who by this time was in her last year of boarding school, took her summer break at home. I saw a more relaxed, even smiling, Chantal then, and could only envy her having the good fortune to be away from our house for months at a time.

While I always looked forward to seeing Chantal, even better that summer was the fact that my father had moved out of the house. He had grown tired of Valentine and had taken up with Yvonne, a much younger woman; he left everyone behind and moved into an apartment in downtown Kigali, doing us all, except Valentine, a big favor. For her part, Valentine prayed for him and asked God to return him to her, even, or especially, when she came down with a heart attack, and he refused to come to her aid.

About a month later, my father's relationship with Yvonne became strained. For one thing, she had gotten pregnant, and my father didn't want her to have the baby. He had already fathered a lot children (by three different women), and didn't like any of them, so he certainly didn't want another one. My father was also growing tired of fighting with her; although she was 25 years younger than he, she didn't hesitate to stand up to him. So he told her the relationship was over.

It was January 1994 when he came back home. At first, his plan was to pick up some paperwork and then return to his apartment downtown, but while he was home, Yvonne came by looking for him. She arrived in the midst of an argument between my father and Chantal, who was home from school break, and me. He was being his usual tyrannical self, telling us that in Africa women weren't "allowed" to talk in front of a man, and the two of us saying that that was ludicrous, that we knew his religious conversion was nothing but a sham and that he hadn't changed at all, other than the fact that he was no longer hitting us, but that that was only because he was older and also that, at 17 and 14, Chantal and I could now defend ourselves. We also told him that Rwanda was a Catholic country, not a Muslim one where women had no voice.

It soon became clear that my father was intending to move back to the house, a plan that no one other than he liked. Even my stepbrothers Adrien, who was nine, and Placide, who was almost nine, told him they didn't want him back. "You beat us all the time," they said. "You're not nice to us. We are happy without you." I was proud of those boys for standing up to their awful father even though it didn't carry any weight with him as he moved back just as he said he would.

For the first week, everyone ignored him. I remember one day Chantal and I were in the family room, talking and having a fun time. When he appeared and came to sit with us, she and I got up and left. That may sound cruel, but it was how we felt, and, besides, what he had done to us for years was the real cruelty, not our behavior. Everyone in the house was extremely upset that the friendly feeling we had enjoyed during his absence had now been turned on its head. "Why did you come back?" Chadrac, the 7-year-old, said, his lament speaking for us all.

Still professing his Christian beliefs, my father resumed his church-going life, but this time he was more relaxed about it and didn't force his routine, such as getting up at dawn to pray with him, on the rest of us. In becoming involved in the church, I was hoping to improve as a person, to forget my past and, if I were lucky, to find even a scrap of happiness. I would fast for days, pray and read my Bible. For me, the church became a refuge as well as a place to get closer to God. It also brought me new friends because most of the people I knew who were my age were Christians, and I now had more in common with them than when I was in my "atheist phase." I started going to Bible study one day a week. I would sleep with my Bible and began devoting more and more of my life to my faith. Believing in God helped me begin to put my anger behind me and directed me to being nicer, more relaxed and more respectful, especially to my brothers, whom I grew to love and tried to be help whenever I could.

For the first time in my life I started believing in myself and putting my trust in God. I remember my aunt's saying she couldn't comprehend how much of the Bible I knew or how much I prayed. "Kids your age don't have time for God," she said.

Then Valentine said, "Oh, Christine does!" Today, after the seemingly endless years of fighting and the bitterness and unhappiness she brought into my life, Valentine is my best friend. I know that is hard to believe, but it's true. After all the pain, I never dreamed she would be a good, loving parent to me and Chantal. I have to give her credit; she made enormous changes in her life and never gave up on herself.

No matter how successful I was in reestablishing friendly relations with Valentine and my brothers, I found that it was impossible to bring myself to forgive my father, my previous promise to him and my strong Christian beliefs notwithstanding. The pain and the damage were just too great. Even so, my faith in God and his love for me gave me hope that better days lay ahead. However, as events would prove, that hope was tragically misplaced. My country would soon collapse into cataclysm.

5

THE MASSACRE: MY NEIGHBORS, MY ENEMY, MY KILLERS AND THE HATE OF PEOPLE DURING THE CIVIL WAR AS THE WORLD STOOD BY AND WATCHED, AND "NO ONE WANTED TO GET INVOLVED"

It is impossible to accurately describe the psychological makeup of a person who is your neighbor and best friend for years who over-night becomes a bloodthirsty murderer motivated by one goal: to hunt you down and kill you. People you trusted the most turning into unrecognizable fiends, people who didn't just want you dead in a theoretical sense but who went into the streets, hunted you down and murdered you, the more grisly the killing, as far as they were concerned, the better.

Rwanda is a small country situated in central and east Africa with a population made up primarily of two ethnic groups, Tutsi and Hutu. As I mentioned earlier, as result of pronouncements made by Belgium when it controlled Rwanda, the Tutsis were in power at the time of the country's independence in 1962. Their hold over the government was short lived, however, as, soon, the Hutus took power and exiled many of the previously empowered Tutsis. In 1990, a rebel group consisting mainly of Tutsis invaded the country, initiating a civil war that eventually resulted in a ceasefire between the warring parties. The truce did not last. When, on the evening of April 7, 1994, a plane carrying Rwandan president Juvénal Habyarimana, a Hutu, (and Burundian Pres. Cyprien Ntaryamira) was shot down and he was killed, the country descended into chaos. The Rwandan genocide had begun.

The hatred exposed in the genocide had its roots deep in Rwandan society and history. Years before, I remember when our Hutu neighbors would sing songs proclaiming their hatred of Tutsis and how they would kill them all. My father and Valentine, who were both Tutsi, were frightened at these portents and would lock the gates to our house and tell us children to hide under our beds.

The Interahamwe, the Rwandan paramilitary group formed around this time, held meetings and made plans to kill Tutsis and sometimes would knock on your door just to tell you how soon they would be back to kill you. My father, wanting to protect us, made plans to construct hiding places in our house, including a false ceiling and a bunker in the back yard. But he never got to finish them as events in April quickly spiraled out of control: literally within hours of President Habyarimana's assassination, the mass slaughter of Tutsis had begun.

With the situation becoming direr by the day, our father told all of us what to do if were attacked—that we should hide and stay together if possible. One morning on his way home from church he saw dozens of men on the street carrying machetes drenched in blood. He tried to ignore them, but as that was just a few days after President Habyarimana had been killed, that was an impossibility, as there was terror everywhere. The Hutu gangs saw my father and said, "Hey, cockroach, soon we will pay you a visit," and pointed their machetes at him. He continued walking, knowing if he ran, they would kill him. When he got home, he locked the house and told everyone to stay inside. He then called us into the living room and said from now on we were to stay in the house, keep all the lights off at night and make no noise during the day.

We lived just a few houses away from Pres. Habyarimana's daughter and were surrounded by Hutu militias who worked there as security. All my life I had heard my family talking about what had happened in 1959 during the Rwandan Revolution, when Hutus killed thousands of Tutsis and forced over 100,000 of them to flee the country. Nyiradegeya, my grandmother on my father's side, had always said that would happen again. She was right; it did, only to an extent that would have been incomprehensible to her or anyone else.

The Hutus blamed the death of President Habyarimana on the Tutsis, but even today no one can say with certainty who was responsible, with some claiming a rogue element of the Hutus was behind the killing while others insist the current president, Paul Kagame, ordered it. What everyone does agree on is that the assassination was the catalyst for the ensuing slaughter over the course of approximately 100 days of 800,000 to one million Tutsi and politically moderate Hutu, who were killed in well-planned attacks on the orders of the provisional government. So it was that on April 7, my life and the life of my country changed forever.

I was only 15 when the genocide began. Over the course of the next three months, I would witness and live through a personal hell, climaxing in an enforced stay in the hospital where I lay in a coma and on the verge of death for two months.

My first exposure to the slaughter happened on Day One of the genocide, April 7. I heard Alina, my friend who lived next door, screaming for help and saw two crazed men with blood-spattered machetes chasing her. She tried to climb the concrete wall between our houses, but before I could grab her and help her over, the men seized her and killed her before my very eyes with a machete. Then they turned to me and said our house was next, that they were coming to kill us all. In shock, I decided to run inside to warn my family and tell them what had happened, but I was too late. The house was already under invasion by a gang of Hutus. Realizing it was too dangerous to go inside, I hid in the bushes in the back yard, where, looking around, I could see smoke rising from houses in the neighborhood that had been set on fire by the death squads. Then I heard one of the attackers yell to my father, "You must choose the way you want to die. Number one is by machete. Number two, if you want me to shoot you, you will have to buy a bullet and pay me, and I will shoot you in the head."

I found out later what happened after that. Nyiradegeya tried to talk to the killers to get them to leave, but they didn't want to hear from their victims, so they cut her in her stomach with their machetes in front of the whole family, including my little brothers. Turning to them, one killer said, "See? This is what happens to all cockroaches like you." Then Fabrice started to cry, and when one member of the gang told him to stop but he didn't, he got angry and decided to kill him. "You are annoying me," he said. "I will shut you up with my machete." Poor Fabrice, that beautiful child, was only five. Even though, thank God, the animals didn't kill everyone, Valentine was tied up on the ground and raped, and my father was beaten and forced to watch her being assaulted and Fabrice and his mother slaughtered. It was a nightmare, and it was happening in homes, neighborhoods, towns and cities all over Rwanda.

I didn't know what to do. I couldn't go inside the house, so I waited till it was dark and went to the house of some neighbors who had been nice to me before. But they told me to go away or they would kill me if I came back.

I was so scared I could hardly breathe, my chest on fire and my mind a blank. I ran back to my house and hid again in the bushes. With my neighbors threatening to kill me, I realized I had only one choice: to leave my neighborhood, go on the run and take my chances.

Because of the fighting, there was no electricity or running water. It was dark and all the telephones were dead and, of course, there were no cell phones in those days. With no power, there was, for all practical purposes, no communication. The Hutus ordered everyone to stay in their houses, which made it easier for them to find their victims. They made lists of the homes they wanted to attack. Everything was planned and coordinated. And methodically carried out.

That night, while hiding at my house, I heard a familiar voice and realized it was that of a man who many times had raped my neighbor, in front of her husband. She would come by our house crying and tell Valentine what had happened; this was a long time before the genocide, but I still recognized that man's voice. Now he was in our house, telling my father that he knew there were two "mixed" girls living there. I found out later that he asked my father to "produce" Chantal and me and when my father refused, he kicked and bloodied him.

Chantal, at least, was safe. Or so I thought. She was at her boarding school in Ntendezi, far away from Kigali. But, as tensions had already worsened in Rwanda, the school had announced via radio a few days before the massacre began that parents should come for their children as quickly as possible. My father knew it was suicide to drive on the streets of Kigali, so he sneaked out of the house and asked a man who had a son at the school to help Chantal. My father hoped the man could somehow get her to the Congo and safety, but the man was unable to offer assistance. Just when it seemed there was no hope of rescuing Chantal, the parents of a classmate of hers who lived near the school took her in and hid her, unbeknownst to us. As the massacre continued to gather force, a Hutu gang invaded the parents' house looking for Tutsis. Ransacking the premises, they came literally within inches of finding Chantal, who was almost suffocating in her hiding place, before leaving without their quarry. Chantal owed her life to this brave family. They were Hutu, but they didn't care what a person's ethnicity was and showed they were willing to risk their lives for a friend, no matter her background.

The family, the Mugabes, then decided to leave their house and try to make it to the Congo. As they prepared, they knew there was only one way they would have even the slightest chance of saving Chantal, and that was to hide her. But where? They decided to wrap her in a mattress and put her on top of their car with their luggage. It was a long, five-hour drive to the border in normal times. Now, with roadblocks everywhere and roving gangs of machete- and gun-wielding Hutus stopping traffic at the slightest whim or suspicion, the drive would take more than twice as long. Chantal could expect to have to stay wrapped in that mattress, scarcely able to breathe, the entire time.

Bodies of dead Rwandans of all ages lined the roads and highways, and Chantal's rescuers were stopped over and over by paramilitaries looking for Tutsis. Each time, the car was searched, and each time the family, which included three small children, stayed calm as the Hutu looked in the trunk, asked questions and scrutinized papers. More than once, the Mugabes were robbed.

As the drive went on, Chantal became more and more desperate. Confined as she was, breathing was extremely hard, and she couldn't stretch or relieve herself. This terrible state of affairs continued for hours. How she survived, I can only guess. To me, it showed how strong and determined she was. Now it was dark, and the family was looking for a place to rest when they were stopped by a pickup truck loaded with paramilitaries. They were drunk and high on drugs and flourished machetes covered in blood. They ordered everybody out of the vehicle and went through the entire interior, finding nothing, but making off with all the food and what remained of the other possessions in the car and trunk. Then one of the killers asked his fellow militiamen if anyone wanted the "skinny, ugly mattress" on the roof. One of them touched it and said his mattress was better, so he left it where it was. Incredibly and by the closest of calls, Chantal had survived yet another brush with death.

Mr. Mugabe wasn't nearly so fortunate. Shortly after Chantal's close call with the paramilitaries, he decided to stop for gas at a nearby village. But first, knowing that Chantal was miserable in the mattress and worried she was at risk of discovery, he got her down from the car and told her to hide in the woods, saying he would come back for her soon. In the village, though, he was attacked and killed by a gang of Hutus. Hysterical, his wife raced with her children to pick up Chantal and, she hoped, get to the Congolese border. The woman, Theresa, asked Chantal, now inside the car, to get out a map for directions, but, as they were afraid of turning on the interior lights, Chantal had to sit on the floor and read the map with a small flashlight she had brought with her. The drive seemed to take forever, but eventually they made it to the border. Having gotten this far, Chantal once again thought of how the Mugabes were putting their lives at risk—were *losing* their lives—in part to save her. She wept for their bravery and sacrifice.

As the car approached the crossing, Chantal saw many paramilitaries—appearing to number in the thousands—patrolling the area and stopping vehicles and pedestrians. Wearing dirty, blood-stained clothes, they were armed with machetes or automatic weapons. It was then that Theresa told her children to hide in the trunk, but Chantal went in first. Saying she would leave the keys in the car, Theresa said. "If they take me away, I want one of you to drive the car across the border as fast as you can." She told her children she loved them and to stay together. They said they were not leaving her, but she said, "It's the only way you will survive." Turning to Chantal, she asked her, as the oldest, to promise to take good care of the children and keep them together. "Please," she said to Chantal and her children. "My husband— your father—is dead, and if I have to die to protect all of you, then that is what I will do." Everyone was panic stricken and in tears.

The guards on the Congo side of the border could only look on in horror as Theresa stayed behind to an uncertain fate at the hands of her captors. Thanks to her bravery and sacrifice, Chantal and the children were now safe. But they were also alone, hungry, lost and homeless. They didn't want to go too far from the crossing in case their mother managed to escape her captors and cross to safety.

At first, they slept in their car by the side of a busy road, but then a Congolese man found them and offered to help. He drove them to his house in their car, where he promised them they would be safe.

During the day the children and Chantal would walk to the border to see if Theresa was there, but it was to no avail. Then one morning when they were trying to find someone kind enough to feed them, they saw a woman who appeared to have been beaten and who was crying. The woman, speaking Rwandan, told Chantal and the others that she had just escaped from a house across the border where a lot of women were being held, saying that there was one poor woman whose name she didn't know whose husband had been killed and who was crying for her children who had escaped into the Congo. The woman told the children that this woman was tied up, repeatedly raped, injured and near death. She said the woman didn't care about the violence against her, that all that mattered was that her children were safe, that that possibility was what was keeping her alive.

Chantal's friends said, "Oh, God, that's our mother! She didn't die!" She was locked up but still alive! Chantal and the children, knowing that the border was only a five-minute walk away, wanted to try to sneak across after dark and rescue her, but the woman who had escaped told them it was too dangerous. So all they could do was wait and hope.

During that time, Chantal and the children spent their days crying and their nights sleeping in their car in the Congolese man's yard. At least they were safe. Painfully for Chantal, she didn't know of my whereabouts or safety or that of the rest of our family; and painfully for us, neither did we know of hers.

One day soon after hearing the woman's story about Theresa, Chantal woke up in the car as she always did. Gazing from a window, she saw a woman walking in her direction. She blinked. Could it be? she asked herself. She screamed. "Children, wake up! It's your mother!" It was nothing less than a dream become real. They all ran to each other and collapsed to the ground, arms entwined, tears flowing. No one could believe this was really happening.

Theresa's escape couldn't have been scripted in a more dramatic and unlikely fashion if it had been written for a movie. It turned out that a Hutu militia man had tried to drag her into the woods to rape her. Desperate, and sick of the repeated attacks on her, she grabbed the man's gun, shot him while he was assaulting her and took his weapon. She then staggered to the border unimpeded because it was dark and raining and most of the militia men were either drunk or sleeping. The next day, the Hutus found the guard dead, his weapon missing and Theresa gone. At about that same time, Theresa and her children were being reunited after fearing they would never see each other again. Listening to Theresa's story, all I could think was that it was a gift from

God. Or Hollywood.

Because she had been subjected to so many assaults, Theresa was in bad shape, and she went to the hospital for treatment. She had a broken arm and other problems, but eventually she recovered, at least physically. She, her three children and Chantal were then relocated to a refugee camp near the border where they stayed till the genocide ended. They had nothing, only their car, which Theresa wanted to keep as a remembrance of her husband.

Back at home and running on pure adrenaline from the shock of seeing my family murdered, I somehow managed to get away before the Hutus could come back and kill me. As I jumped over the concrete wall behind our house, one Hutu saw me, but I was able to outrun him and, at least for the moment, escape injury, or worse. It was raining and many houses in my neighborhood were on fire or already destroyed, so I didn't know where to go. I was wearing only shorts and a shirt and no shoes. I thought I was going crazy and didn't know what to do with myself. I hid out and slept in bushes that night and didn't feel safe, so I decided to see if some people I knew who lived in a different part of Kigali would help me and not tell me to go away the way my neighbors had. I knew I was risking my life by being out on the street, especially during daylight, which I tried to avoid, but the sad fact was I had no choice but to expose myself to the omnipresent danger.

I was all by myself and had to be strong or face the consequences. The house I was looking for was about two miles away, but in the dark and rain, the two miles might as well have been 200. Knowing what would happen to me if I gave up, I was determined to keep going till I found a safe haven with those people—my friend Brigitte, her brother Eric and their family.

Bodies and blood were everywhere. I was, almost literally, knee deep in it. I had to watch where I walked to avoid stumbling over the dead, who seemed to outnumber the living. There were men, women, children, even infants; everyone was fair game for the death squads and their savagery. At one point, as I was getting nearer to Brigitte's neighborhood, I was stopped short by a low moaning sound that appeared to be aimed at me. A woman who had somehow survived a mass killing was trapped in a pile of bodies and asking for help. Still traumatized by my family's slaughter and what I was seeing around me, I was torn between wanting to help and wanting to run for my life. I decided to try to help but told the woman that I was scared. She said she was scared, too. I don't know how, but I managed to pull all those bodies off and help her get out. She thanked me profusely and then said that her husband and children were missing and she didn't know if they had escaped or been killed. She was hysterical, calling for her children and asking me where I was going. I told her I had no idea, that people I had known were turning their backs on me. At that moment, I realized I felt abandoned by the world. I hugged the woman and told her that I was sure she would find her children, that they were probably hiding somewhere. It was the culmination of the most frightening, sickening, horrifying day of my life. For now.

It had become clear that the UN peacekeeping force was there only to help expatriates, not Rwandans. I heard a UN peacekeeper say they were only taking white people and ask Rwandans to keep their distance. He said those were his orders. But if they weren't there to help the desperate Tutsi and Hutu victims, I said to myself, why *were* they there? I found out later that that was a question many people in other countries were also asking. It seemed Rwandans, a poor, black people, were being abandoned by the world, left to be wiped out by genocidal executioners given free rein to destroy an entire country.

I saw the white UN trucks moving down the streets as people were dying or getting killed and doing nothing, as though out for a Sunday drive. One day I saw a car filled with frantic Rwandans following one of those trucks hoping to get through the Interahamwe roadblocks in order to save their lives. When a Hutu asked the peacekeepers if the car was with them, they said no. All the peacekeepers had to do was say yes and possibly save the lives of innocent people. But, of course, those weren't their orders.

On that occasion, after the UN trucks went through, the Interahamwe asked the people in the car to show their identity cards.

One of the killers said, "If you are Hutu, you are my brothers. If you are Tutsi, we will kill you. This is Hutu land; we hate Tutsis." When one of the men in the car didn't have his card, a Hutu with a machete said he was going to kill him. But the man's friend begged him not to; then the Hutu gave the friend his machete and ordered him to kill the man, his best friend.

He started crying and screaming, saying to his friend, who by now had been forced to lie on the ground, "I can't do this. I love you. I cannot kill you; you are a brother to me." He begged the Hutu to spare his friend and told them he hadn't done anything wrong. Suddenly, another Hutu got mad and shot the man's friend in the head. He died at his sobbing friend's feet.

The man whose friend had been shot kept telling him to get up but his friends in the car said they had to go "before they kill us, too." All the people in the car had Hutu papers, which is why they weren't killed, but the man who was shot was killed only because he had lost or forgotten his or was a Tutsi and was trying to hide the fact. Your ID card was your life. Whether you had one or not and which ID card it was determined whether you lived or died. If it said Tutsi, then you might as well throw it away because it would condemn you to death.

The peacekeepers were under siege from helpless Rwandans whose only hope was with the men wearing the white UN helmets. Sometimes, even, the UN forces (formally known as the United Nations Assistance Mission for Rwanda, or UNAMIR) would shoot their weapons into the air to disperse the *victims*, so many there were begging for help. The peacekeepers would then drive away in their empty trucks, as the people they were all but consigning to death shouted *You are saying you will leave us to die?*

Houses were burning and people were dying, but the UN did nothing. (I found out later that UNAMIR peacekeepers, "acting as individuals and as a group did manage to save the lives of thousands of Tutsis in and around Kigali and the few areas of UN control," according to an entry in Wikipedia. While this action was laudable and certainly welcomed, it was not enough to save the lives of up to a million other Rwandans.) The fault wasn't with the UN; it was with the member nations that limited the organization's mandate for reasons that, in essence, were meant to protect their self-interest, and if hundreds upon hundreds of thousands of innocent people died as a result, what was it to them?

At least the RPF (the Rwanda Patriotic Front) was trying to help the Tutsis. Eventually, the RPF would take control of the country, starting with Kigali on July 4, 1994, and the entire country by July 18, but not before the genocide had taken its terrible toll.

One thing I could never understand was how the Hutus seemed to *enjoy* the killing. To say they were bloodthirsty would be to offer up a major understatement. You would see them killing and laughing, as if taking the lives of unarmed, innocent people, even infants, of neighbors, friends and entire families were sport and they'd won the top prize. Which, until the RPF fought back, I guess they had.

If the Hutu were gleeful in their killing, they were, or came to be, angry as well. When, as the RPF retaliated, their fortunes began to change, they turned ever more on their own, searching out those Hutu trying to help their fellow Rwandans, whatever their ethnicity, and killing them with neither justice nor mercy. So it came to be that untold thousands of the victims of the genocide were Hutu men, women and children.

As the killing went on unabated, the dead along the streets of Kigali and other Rwandan cities, towns and villages continued to pile up until there were bodies beyond counting. For the survivors, witnessing this carnage was the most hellish experience imaginable, and I still have nightmares about those mutilated, bloated, fly-infested bodies seemingly everywhere.

During the genocide, radio, especially the government-owned RTLM, was used by extremist Hutu conspirators to mobilize the Hutu majority, to coordinate the killings and to ensure that the plans for extermination were faithfully executed, which they were in hundreds of small villages and towns across the country where Tutsis and Hutus had lived together peacefully, as well as in Kigali and other cities.

With the systematic and relentless attacks, you would see thousands of people in the streets, many wandering aimlessly, in shock, carrying whatever belongings they could salvage, people of all ages, including children now orphaned, having abandoned or been forced from the homes that had been their only, if insecure, refuge from the killing. Amid this outpouring of desperate souls, many Tutsis tried to "pass" as Hutu to avoid discovery by the Interahamwe, by, for example, pretending to talk like Hutus or, emerging from their hiding places after weeks or months, mixing in with them. Even though the Interahamwe often based their live-or-die decisions on physical appearance—if you were tall, they decided, you were a Tutsi, and killed—to me you could put a Hutu and a Tutsi side by side and not tell the difference. They all looked the same. Some Hutus were tall, and some Tutsis were short. And all Rwandans, Hutu and Tutsi alike, spoke the same language. It was the instigators of the genocide who created the false divisions and hatred between Hutu and Tutsi. By far the majority of the Rwandan people got along well with one another.

I often wonder, as I recall the horrors of the genocide, what would have happened to the Tutsis and supportive Hutus if the RPF hadn't been there to save us. In my worst fears, I think we would have all been killed, every last one. As it was, two million Rwandans of every ethnicity were forced to flee the country to avoid annihilation or because they had become homeless, a tragedy that often gets overlooked in accounts of the slaughter.

The Hutu killers would search homes for their victims and sing songs of death to the Tutsis. When they found Tutsis, as they murdered them, they would sing, "Kill them! Don't let them go! We are cleaning out all the Tutsis!"

I was hiding, starving and cold, yet, thanks to the power of God, I survived to tell my story.

Some members of my father's family lived in Nyamata, a city south of Kigali of about 115,000 people at the time of the genocide. It was a place where everyone seemed to know everyone, especially those who were Catholic, most of whom went to the same church every Sunday.

When the killing in Nyamata started, everyone rushed to the church, thinking it a place to take refuge, but they were horribly mistaken. My cousin Nyiramana, who spent several days at the church, told me that when the Hutu militia showed up, a priest betrayed the Tutsi townspeople who had trusted him and did nothing while the innocents were murdered. With only a few exceptions, everyone who had taken refuge in that church was killed.

Priests aided and abetted the killing elsewhere in Rwanda as well. Probably the most notorious collaborator was Athanase Seromba, a priest in Nyange parish in the western part of the country. With his active participation, the Interahamwe and other militia members, armed with machetes, guns, rifles and bulldozers, encircled his church, trapping inside the more than 1,500 Tutsi who had been told it was a safe haven. The violence began on April 15, culminating, on the morning of April 16, in the killing of some 2,000 persons amid the wholesale destruction of the church. Seromba is serving a life sentence in prison for his crimes against the innocent people of Nyange. It is one of the few cases of justice for the people of Rwanda, living and dead.

In Nyamata and Bugesera, the latter the district in which Nyamata is located, unlike the rest of Rwanda where the Hutu dominated, the population was evenly split between Hutu and Tutsi. But then a mayor in the district, a Hutu, was killed, and the Hutu leaders targeted all the Tutsis for revenge. After the genocide, a terrible silence fell over Nyamata, one defined by the utter absence of people going about their daily lives. Nyiramana, who has lived in Nyamata all her life, told me how the birds would eat so much fruit from the trees that they were unable to fly. There were no people around to scare them off.

Nyiramana suffered horribly in the genocide. She lost part of her body, one leg and one arm, and her children and her husband, all of whom died in the church massacre. She was lonely, sick and in pain. She had nowhere to go. All she wanted was to die. She had lost her loved ones and was disabled for the rest of her life, all because of who she was, a Tutsi. She hated herself and tried to commit suicide many times.

Like so many others in Rwanda, I was scared all the time. My only wish was to find a way to leave my country and go back to Europe, to my grandmother, and never come back to Africa, but that was a fantasy. I was worried about Chantal and didn't know if she was wounded or even alive. I was frightened and lonely and saw no way out. I felt my life was over. I *wanted* my life to be over. Even though I had survived so far, I felt that God wasn't listening to me no matter how hard I prayed.

All the while, I ran for my life. I ran and ran till I couldn't run anymore. With no shoes and bleeding and in pain from cuts on the bottoms of my feet, I struggled even to walk. I was constantly on the lookout for a better hiding spot. My family lived in the most devastated part of Kigali, where many people had been killed. In that part of town it didn't matter if you knew everyone because all your Hutu neighbors were looking for you and wanting to rob and kill you and steal from your house and burn it down. My father had a dirt bike, a Toyota family car and fairly expensive furnishings in his house at that time. After the house was invaded, some neighbors went there and took our furniture and my father's dirt bike. It didn't matter to them that people had been killed and their bodies were still in the house or that the house had been half destroyed. All they wanted was your possessions. These were people you had lived next to and played with and trusted all your life. That's what made it so sad. There was one man my family had known whom I saw during the genocide. He had gone from being a normal, well-liked neighbor to a wild-looking, intoxicated, red-eyed fanatic with a bloody machete who said he wanted nothing more than "to kill all the Tutsis."

I remember one time I was scared because of dogs and voices around my hiding spot. In a panic, I started running, but I soon realized I was heading in the wrong direction—toward the roadblocks, not away from them. Try to imagine the utterly cold fear of knowing that your life is about to end. I decided my only chance was to hope somehow that the human animals lying in wait would take pity on me and not, figuratively, or maybe literally, tear me limb from limb. To hope that this day was not my day to die. I was surrounded by killers and dead people. With no escape, I could only hope—pray— that if my time had come, it would be at the end of a gun and not a machete. Please, I prayed, anything but a machete.

Try, for a minute, to imagine that fear. Now try to imagine that you're only 14 years old.

An Interahamwe with a machete said to me, "You! Wait there! I'll be back in a minute. I'm going to kill this other cockroach first."

I was standing with people who had their Tutsi identity cards. At first, I thought they were stupid to keep them. But then I realized that not having a card could also cost you your life. I didn't have a card, but, as a minor not required to have one, I had hoped to use that provision to plead for my life. On the other hand, having skin that was so much lighter than that of black Rwandans, along with being tall and thin, doomed me, I thought, my chance for survival being nonexistent.

Listening to the crazed people on RTLM urging them on in their heinous pursuit, the militia men were always on edge and ready to kill. As I approached the roadblock, I knew there was no chance to turn back, that in minutes I would be food for the dogs. All during the genocide, the announcers on RTLM bragged about body counts and how many children had been raped. "Get your machetes. It's time to kill the Tutsis," they screamed. They would say that the graves weren't full yet, that it was time for the Hutus to get up in the morning and go to work killing the Tutsis. The Interahamwe were poor, so the rich Hutu would buy them beer and food and tell them to keep killing. Those who didn't kill would rob and steal; they would strip the victims' houses, taking furnishings, wiring, windows, doors, even roofs. They would roam the streets and take jewelry, money and anything else of value from the bodies piled up on every corner. Some of the most deranged Hutus even killed their own family members if they thought they were being too supportive of the Tutsis or if they were Tutsis themselves—and then steal their possessions. At the roadblock, I was forced to sit by the road and await my fate. But then the killer with the machete was distracted for a minute, and that was all the time I needed to make a run for it. Once again, I had beaten the odds.

I hate thinking about the killings—the people, friends and family I lost who died screaming and tortured. Yet they are impossible *not* to think about. It has taken me almost 20 years to recover my sanity and equilibrium, through therapy, my faith and the love of my husband and son.

There were so many atrocities. I remember once when a woman tried to run back to her burning house to save her four-year-old son. She had taken refuge in a church with many other women and children when someone told her that her house was on fire. She panicked and screamed about her son being there, but an Interahamwe wouldn't let her leave, and the boy died, probably burned alive in the arson. The Interahamwe had said they sent the people to the church, a Catholic church that I used to attend, to protect them. But they later set the church on fire and killed untold numbers of innocents. At least the child's mother didn't have to live with the pain of her son's execution.

As the church burned, the Hutu killers laughed, danced and sang, assaulting any Tutsis who managed to escape the inferno.

Where I was hiding, close to that church, there were other fleeing Tutsis, like me, crying inconsolably, holding our heads down, sick at the sound—a sound too awful for words— of the people screaming as they were being burned alive. At that time, I saw a woman I knew, a Tutsi who was trying to pass as Hutu, and I foolishly left my hiding place to ask her about my father and Valentine. When she saw me, she started yelling to the Interahamwe that I was a Tutsi and not to let me go to distract them so she could get through the roadblock. I turned and ran my fastest, not even thinking about my throbbing feet, and, thank God, outran the militia men to live at least one more day.

It being too risky to sleep on the street and chance discovery, that night, still wearing only a shirt and shorts in the cold and wet and still without shoes, I found a "safe" place in which to sleep: a tree. The next morning I climbed down and, after looking around, came to the frightening realization that I was lost. At that very moment, a group of men saw me and gave chase. Armed with machetes, they were young and fast and would have caught me if not for the fact that while I was running I fell into a hole, causing them to lose sight of me. Even though there were spiders and snakes in the hole, I told myself I was fortunate as I listened to my would-be killers saying, "I can't believe we lost that chicken. She's lucky. I would have chopped her head off."

At terrible times like those, my faith was tested as never before. I found myself doubting, if not the existence of God, then the existence of him in my life, while simultaneously rejoicing in his determination to keep me alive. In the end, I now can say, belief won out over doubt.

While I was still in my hole, a band of Hutus showed up with dogs to hunt for people, saying they hoped they would find more "cockroaches" to kill. These were hardline Hutus, members of the National Republican Movement for Democracy and Development (MRND) that had backed President Habyarimana and organized the genocide in the wake of his assassination. They were very loud, and every time they found some "suspicious" people, they would demand their IDs. There was this one man they stopped who they said was "the guy they were talking about on the radio and who everyone is looking for." They told him to sit on the ground and almost before you would think it possible, a Hutu swung his machete at the man's neck and he fell over on his back, dead, his head separated from his body. The Hutu then abducted his wife and children. If they survived, only God knows.

6

HUTU KILLERS EVERYWHERE AND NOWHERE TO HIDE

All this time it was hard for me even to think. I had given up on finding Brigitte and her family in the other neighborhood, meaning I had nowhere to go and was scared I wouldn't find anyone who felt sorry enough for me to protect me. Minors, who as I say weren't required to have identity papers, were judged as to their ethnicity by their appearance. One ridiculous Hutu who stopped me said, "I can tell what you are by smelling you. You are Tutsi and as you know we are killing Tutsis. We hate Tutsis, so if you lie to me I will kill you anyway." I swore to him that I was Hutu and not Tutsi. Of course everyone denied being Tutsi. When I begged the man to let me go, he said, "Shut up and take off your clothes." I didn't want to make him mad, so I took off my clothes and stood naked in front of a group of Interahamwe while that man smelled me, sniffing my neck and saying I smelled like a Tutsi. Then one of the Hutus said, "I don't have time for this. I will ask you one question, and I need an answer. When was the last time you took a shower?"

While I was being interrogated, I saw some women sitting by the side of the road. The Hutu had just killed their husbands, and one of the women was crying for her family. But another woman kept looking at me as though she wanted to tell me something. Then the Hutu man said to me I looked as if I'd been living in the jungle. "You smell bad, girl, and you're covered with mud." When I didn't say anything to him, he started hitting me in the head, but just then a big commercial truck showed up and got his attention and that of his fellow killers. They ran over to the driver and asked him what he had inside the truck. He said he didn't know and that the truck belonged to his boss.

The Interahamwe started climbing into the back of the truck where they found a lot of people huddling under canvas tents. They told them to get out and show their IDs, so everybody got out, and then the Hutus told them to line up—men, women, children and babies. Then the Hutu started hitting them with their guns and hands. My attention was diverted by the old woman, who said that the Hutu had confiscated my clothes to take them for their children and wives, the same as they had done with other women and girls.

In a few minutes, one of the Interahamwe came to me with a bloody machete and said, "You look like you are ready to die. Do you want me to kill you now? Or do you want to wait?" I looked down, deathly afraid to make eye contact with him, when his friends called him to come to the truck. Realizing that if I hesitated I would be killed, I took the opportunity to run. I thought if you are going to kill me, you will have to catch me first.

I was naked, but I didn't let that stop me. I ran for a very long time, until I got tired and couldn't run anymore. Wary and afraid, I looked back, but no one was following me. I knew the Hutu were busy killing those poor people from the truck. I couldn't believe that no one had shot at me or tried to catch me. Irrational thoughts came to mind, such as the fact that I had managed to escape my killers time and again and thus proved my father wrong when he said I was stupid. After all, I was proving that I could use my brain as well as my strength to outwit grown men. I hoped, again, irrationally, given the crisis, that I would have the chance to tell my father this in person.

The first few weeks of my escape seemed to go on forever, pain and fear unending. When I wasn't trying desperately to avoid the

Hutu gangs or find something to eat, I would think about my younger self and say so what if I die now since my life has been so miserable. In tears, I would think about how my selfish, nasty, sick father, the man I wished would burn in hell, had destroyed my life and that with everyone in my family dead, most terribly Chantal, there was no longer any reason to live. I was tired, hungry, homeless and despairing beyond telling. But then my survivor instinct would take hold, and I would tell myself never to give up. I would pray, asking God to help me, to somehow show me that he existed and would let me live to see a better life.

More mundanely, all what I wanted now was a pair of shoes and some clothes. I was tired of being naked, and my feet were so sore as to make walking excruciatingly painful. As I was trying to find a place to keep from being discovered by the Hutu, I heard people talking and suddenly found myself standing in front of a group of Tutsis in hiding. When they saw me, they said, oh, my God, you are naked, and one lady gave me a sweater to wear. Another one gave me one of the two skirts she had on. "I will die, anyway," she said, "and don't need it." I was so grateful but also so tired that I couldn't summon the strength even to say thank you.

A man who had lost his entire family said the only way to survive was to get to the border, either to Uganda or the Congo. I had no idea how this man, who had large wounds on his neck and forehead, was able to walk and talk, let alone that he was even alive, and wondered what had happened to him. But in the middle of a massacre, 14-year-olds did not ask such questions. I sat dawn to look at my feet, which were swollen and getting more and more painful. I saw there was a big piece of glass stuck in one of them and, no matter how hard I tried, I couldn't get it out. My other foot looked to be infected. Seeing my condition, one woman asked me how I could walk like that. I said to myself fear can overcome many obstacles. Fortunately, the woman was able to remove the piece of glass, saying she was sorry that there was no medicine to put on the wound. I thanked her and said all I really wanted was a pair of shoes, that if I didn't have shoes, I didn't think I could last. Hearing this, the man who had lost his family gave me his socks, which, even though they were dirty and smelly, I was grateful to have. He then asked me where I was from, and when I told him Remera, he said that that was the worst-hit part of the country. When he asked about my family, I told him that my grandmother and a younger brother had been killed but that I didn't know about anyone else. He said to try not to think about them, that I should think about myself now and that I would find my family someday if they had survived. I told him that that was exactly what I was trying to do, that I would never give up, that if the Hutu wanted to kill me, they would have to catch me first. And I added I would die running before I would let that happen, shoes or no shoes.

The man asked me how old I was. When I said fourteen, he said, "For your age, you're a smart, brave kid." I could hardly believe what I was hearing. "You really think I'm smart?" I said. "I never heard anyone in my family tell me that. Thank you." After informing him of the things Leonard had said about me, I said, "I wish you could tell my father that."

This was around the time that nearly 1,300 people took refuge in the Hotel Des Mille Collines in Kigali, and the manager, Paul Rusesabagina, saved their lives by bribing the Interahamwe with money and alcohol. It was all on the radio, so we had heard about it. We wanted to try to get to the hotel, but then we heard on the radio that the UN was pulling out of Rwanda and that the Hutus were being ordered to not let anyone survive, to kill all the Tutsis, including their children, to search homes, the bushes, the mountains, to kill any and all survivors, so our plans changed, and the people in the group and I decided to go our separate ways and hope for the best.

Soon afterward, in the dark and wet and on my own again, I heard shooting and the sound of people approaching. I started running, not even thinking about my painful feet or how weakened from hunger I had become, when I saw that a woman was behind me. "Wait for me, please," she said. At first I was angry at her because I knew I had a better chance of surviving if I were on my own. But then, I stopped and waited for her. It was then that I found out I had been shot in the leg.

I had felt nothing. I told the woman, "Running is what I do best. I've been running for a month now." Then I asked her, "What happened?" She said that Hutus were shooting at us and then said, "Oh, God. You have blood on you. Did you get shot?" That was when I realized I had been hit.

The woman said she had left her children behind, becoming hysterical. I begged her not to cry and give away our whereabouts, but she couldn't help herself. I hugged her and said, "I'm so sorry." Just as I had been told by the man who gave me his socks, I told her that when this was all over, she would be reunited with her children, even if I knew that with all the killing their survival was a faint hope at best. She was a very strong woman, and she looked at my wound and said it should be cleaned. But there was nothing to clean it with, so I told her I was fine and said that far more important for me was to find some shoes.

Spending a few minutes with this woman and for the first time since I had been running, I felt as if it were a good idea to have someone with me, especially because the woman in question, whose name was Immacuree, was kind and generous. Unfortunately, worried as she was about her children, she cried all the time because she knew it was too dangerous to go back to look for them. I told her how I believed God had saved my life during the massacre and how my father had changed his life and become a Christian (even though I didn't believe him). I also told her how terrible he had been and that if he said he had changed then I believed God would change the situation for Immacuree and me, and that we and our families would survive.

Immacuree interrupted me, whispering that we were being watched. We stopped talking, but she kept looking at me, and I could see in her face that she was frightened. I was, too. I didn't dare speak. In an instant, we both thought we were under attack by the Interahamwe. Some of them were cutting through a cluster of bushes and saying they were sure there were "some Tutsis hiding there." But we didn't move, and the Hutu seemed to be drunk or drugged, luckily for us, and, not seeing anyone, soon moved on. All I could think was that God was by my side still, and that now he was watching over two of his children.

Over and over during the trials that were my life, I would pray to God and ask why me? What did I do to deserve this? What is the point of my suffering? When I despaired of my prayers' being answered, I would tell myself that prayers don't always get answered right away, but that doesn't mean they won't eventually be. You must put your faith in God, Christine, I reminded myself, have him in your heart and trust him. I kept telling God during those unspeakable months that he was the only one I trusted, the only one other than my loving sister who had not let me down. I told God I knew he would continue to save me as he had been doing.

The Hutus would resort to anything to kill Tutsis. I well remember one day Immacuree and I heard a couple screaming for help, but we were worried it might be a trap and that a band of Hutus might be waiting to capture and kill us. Instead of helping the couple, Immacuree said we should pray for them, and that is what we did even though it was hard to ignore their desperate cries. But then, we were shocked to see the couple, who had stopped screaming, get up and casually stretch, as if not having a care in the world. To our even greater amazement, a group of Hutus who had been in hiding went to them and said, "I guess we wasted our time. There aren't any Tutsis here." Immacuree was right: it had been a trap, and the only reason we survived was that we hadn't fallen for it. I thanked Immacuree over and over and told her how smart she was to have figured that out and how happy I was that I had listened to her.

During my weeks and months running, my body often betrayed me, especially my digestive tract. With hardly anything to eat, I suffered from stomach pain and nausea. I also had blurred vision. There were lots of abandoned houses, and when I would say to Immacuree that we should stay in one or look for some food, she would say she was too scared to go in. Then I would become scared, too. But she would overcome her fear and go into the house, saying, "I will treat you as one of my children. If I don't come out of that house, at least I will have died helping you!"

One time when she went into a house, she found uncooked rice and old carrots, but the best things she found were a pair of shoes, a warm sweater and a blanket. She covered me with the blanket and laid my head in her lap. Then she went back into the house and cooked the rice, and when I woke up the next morning I had rice to eat and shoes to wear. I told Immacuree that she had saved my life again.

I promised her that if we survived, I would find her and we would be together as a family and that I would help her find her children. She said, "Christine, from now on you are my family." Hearing that someone loved me like that strengthened my will to get through my ordeal.

Immacuree and I were together for many weeks, and whenever I thought about letting my hurt overcome me or felt especially sad, she would give me a hug and tell me we needed to stay strong, to keep moving, that to stop was to ask for trouble. I would often question her about where we were, and she would always say she didn't know. "I've lost track," she would say and ask me, forgetting that I, a 14-year-old girl who had almost never left home, knew nothing of the layout of Kigali. We both continued saying our prayers.

My gunshot wound was getting better by this time, but my feet were causing me so much pain, even with the shoes I was wearing, that I was always on the verge of collapse. Whenever Immacuree would ask about my feet, I would lie, telling her that I had gotten used to the discomfort, because I didn't want her to worry about me or to have to listen to my complaints. But there came a time when the pain got to be too much, and I was worried an infection might set in and kill me. I told Immacuree I needed help and medicine. That beautiful woman said she would never abandon me and that she would carry me, if that was what was required, for as long it took till we found a doctor. "I will never leave you behind like I did my children," she said. Even as she was trying to be so optimistic with me, I knew how sad and guilty she felt about what she feared had become of them.

Immacuree carried me on and off for several days. On one of those days, we saw a woman at a house who was arguing with her husband. He was leaving with a machete, saying he was going "to work" and that if she didn't like it, he would kill her, too. On her way into the house, she saw Immacuree carrying me and offered to feed us, telling us to hurry into her house to keep from being seen.

Immacuree told her I was sick, and if I didn't get help I might die, but the only medicine the woman had was a painkiller. After an hour, she told us we had to leave because her husband, who was Hutu, was out killing Tutsis, and if he returned and found us, he would kill us, no questions asked. Before we left, I told her I was curious about how long it would take to walk to Remera, where I used to live, and she said it was too far to walk. Even in a car, she said, it would take three hours to get there!

Then this lady saw my feet and said now I see why you are sick. Your feet look really bad, and I bet you have an infection. After thinking it over, she changed her mind and said we didn't have to leave and that she would treat my feet. This woman, whom we assumed was Hutu, was nice and caring. But she was worried that if her husband came back and found Immacuree and me there, he would kill us, so she said she would hide us if he came home early. She described her husband as a "bad man, an animal, out there killing innocent people." She said she had made a big mistake marrying into a Hutu family and that, essentially, she had been disowned by her own family. Immacuree wondered aloud if she was "one of us." Are you Tutsi? she asked. The woman said that, yes, she was Tutsi but that all her husband's friends think she is Hutu. "I act Hutu," she said. "If anyone found out I was Tutsi, they would kill me." Immacuree and I looked at each another, and we knew we were thinking the same thing: this dysfunctional household stood for everything tragic that had come to pass in our country.

After we learned that the woman was Tutsi, Immacuree and I were more comfortable with her. She asked us our names and told us hers, Ingabire, and said I would feel better the next day. When she asked if there was anything else I needed, I said only for the pain to go away so

I could walk. She told us that her husband brings clothing and other items home every day from when he and his Hutu friends rob stores and homes. Pointing to a storage room, she said, "I'm sure in those bags over there we will find something for you to wear," but I told her I the only thing I wanted was food and medicine, nothing else.

Ingabire had just told us how bad her husband was, and while she was saying this she had begun to get upset. Then she showed us her feet. I couldn't believe what I was seeing: she had no toes! Crying, she said, "The last time I tried to leave him, this is what he did to me! He chopped my toes off." Immacuree and I were in shock, but as horrible as Ingabire's situation was and as terrible as I felt for her, I felt even worse for myself and Immacuree. At least Ingabire had a roof over her head, and even though her sadistic husband was killing Tutsis, he hadn't killed her. Besides, she not only had a warm and comfortable house, she had clothes and food, necessities Immacuree and I and the thousands of other victims of the massacre had none of.

Ingabire went into the storage room and found some pants and shoes, asking if I wanted sandals. I said no, thank you, but that if she had any socks, I would take those. I didn't want anything from her, especially things that had been stolen from Tutsis, but Immacuree urged me to reconsider, and I realized I needed Ingabire's help to survive. After looking for shoes, she said there were none but that she could get some socks from her husband if I liked. I said no, thank you. I refused to wear socks from my enemy who was killing innocent people although, yes, it was true, I was eating his food. Immacuree knew how my feet were bothering me and how sick I was because, of course, she had been carrying me all this time. She said, "Take the socks, Christine," and so I did.

When Ingabire was trying to decide what to do with us, she saw her husband home for lunch. She quickly hid us in her bedroom and told us to be completely quiet till he left and she came for us. She then went to the kitchen, which was outdoors, and pretended to be alone while she prepared her husband's lunch. Immacuree and I could hear what he was saying to her: that "very soon all the Tutsis will be dead." Ingabire called in from outside and said, "Not all of them. I am Tutsi, too. Will you kill me, also? If you kill me, you will have to kill your children, too." Immacuree and I wanted to cheer her on, but of course we dared not say a thing. We ended up staying in that bedroom for three hours! And for all that time, we knew that even the slightest sound could cost us our lives and probably Ingabire's, too. Making it even harder was the fact that the medicine for my foot was not very effective, and the pain had become unbearable. To make matters worse still, Immacuree and I had to fight the overwhelming need to go to the bathroom. The endless ordeal was a combination of fear and agony combined into one.

Before we were able to come out of hiding, there was a knock on the front door of the house. Immacuree and I could hear that the visitors were friends of Ingabire's husband from the roadblocks, and that they were talking about killing Tutsis. Her husband told Ingabire that his friends were hungry, but Ingabire said she didn't have enough food for them. When he told her to cook more food, Ingabire told him to go back to work. "I'll cook the food and let you know when it's ready," she said. When we heard those words, Immacuree and I knew our misery was finally about to end.

At last the men left and Immacuree and I could come out of the bedroom. However, Ingabire told us we would have to leave before the men came back. Immacuree begged her to let us stay a while longer. "Please," she said. "Christine is sick, and I can't carry her anymore. My back hurts. It's daylight, and we can't let anyone see us." All we wanted was to stay till it got dark. Ingabire said yes, that not only could we stay till it got dark, we could spend the night there. Immacuree and I were so relieved and thankful. "In the morning Christine may feel better and be able to walk on her own," Immacuree said. "I am too old to be carrying her."

We thanked Ingabire for all her help. "We will never forget you," Immacuree said. "You are such a good woman."

When we said to Ingabire that she didn't deserve to live with such an awful man, she told us an all-too-familiar story of a fearful African woman living almost like a slave. "If I leave him he will find a way to kill my family if they are still alive," she said, in tears. "And he will kill me, too." Crying softly, she said, "I wish I were dead. I am tired of living like this. I don't have any friends. My family can't visit and I'm afraid of this man." Sadly, it was a story I had heard, seen—and lived—first hand.

I knew firsthand how hard it is to leave, even as a child, always ending up in the same terrible circumstances because you had no place to go. There was no one to take you in. They were all afraid. And no one had chopped my toes off, either. When I told Ingabire about my horrible life, she tried to make me feel better, saying I was young, that better things would come. "All I want is for you and Immacuree to remember me and my children in your prayers," she said. Immacuree and I were crying for this woman who was so kind, and so undeserving of her pain.

Ingabire wanted to help us even more now and gave us food. But I ate only fruit, politely refusing the meat she offered because I knew the cow had been slaughtered with machetes used to kill people and, even worse, that the owner of the cow had been killed first. By now, my feet, though still sore, were feeling better, thanks to the aspirin Ingabire had given me, and my gunshot wound didn't bother me at all. Immacuree's back was better, too.

We asked Ingabire if there were anywhere we could go, and she said no, that the Interahamwe were everywhere, that it was too danger-ous to be out on the street. She said we could stay with her for a while longer unless her husband got suspicious and that she would pack food for us if that happened and we had to leave. We thanked her again for being so kind.

It turned out that her husband had got into an argument with some of his fellow Hutu killers. They put the idea into his head that maybe Ingabire was Tutsi and was hiding other Tutsis in his house. Then, when they said that maybe he was also on the Tutsis' side, he said if he were, why would he be killing them, and stormed off for home.

Arriving at his house, he complained about the men to Ingabire, who became even more frightened but managed to stay calm, and asked her if she were hiding any Tutsis there. She said no. "I already told you. You don't trust me?" she said. "There's no way I would or even could hide anyone in this house. You would kill them if you found them."

"You are right," he said. "I would."

He said he had told the "dogs" who were accusing him that they could search his house and that they might come that very day to look around and that, in the meantime, he was "taking the day off. It's Sunday, and I don't work on Sunday, so I am just going for a walk."

Ingabire waited to make sure that he was gone, then came to us and told us what had happened and what he had said. "They are coming to search the house," she said. "You must leave now. There is no time to waste. Please go. I am sorry."

We were all scared and crying. Immacuree helped me put on my shoes and lifted me up, as my feet, though better, were still painful. After Ingabire gave us some food, made sure everything was as safe as it could be outside and saw to it that no neighbors were watching, and after we all hugged, Immacuree and I left.

We were in Ingabire's back yard, hiding behind a banana plant, when her husband and his friends came back to search the house. When they didn't find anyone, we heard the men say to him, "This was all a waste of time. Now we can trust you."

We realized how close we had come, yet again, to losing our lives. I am sure we, and Ingabire, would have been killed and chopped to pieces just like all the other innocents if her husband and his fellow Interahamwe had found us. Then, to our surprise, after the others left, we heard him tell Ingabire that because his friends hadn't trusted him, he was "done" and "will not kill Tutsis anymore." From now on, he said, "I will stay here and protect my house, and if they come back, I will kill them." He said he'd been a fool for letting "those idiots" search his house. Immacuree and I could only think: he didn't know how right "those idiots" had been.

Immacuree and I talked about how lucky we were to have met such a kind and generous woman as Ingabire and spoke of how sad we were for her that she was in the situation she was in. It made us even sadder to know that we couldn't help her the same way she had helped us.

We decided to wait till dark to leave the back yard, but because my feet still hurt, I told Immacuree to go on without me, that I would try to find a place to hide until I got better. She looked at me and said, "Are you insane? You are all I have. I've lost my children and my family. We are together, and I will not leave you to die. If we die, we die together."

That night we started moving, slowly at first because of my feet, but then a bit more quickly, although we didn't know where we were going. As we tried to keep out of sight of the Interahamwe, we told each other that we could only hope to meet someone as brave and loving as Ingabire to help us survive.

I kept thinking about Chantal, wondering where she was and if she had been able to escape her pursuers, hoping that she was safe and in a better situation than I was. I was so scared of losing her; she was my best friend, and I didn't know how I would manage if she were gone from my life. I kept my thoughts to myself, though, because Immacuree had lost all her family, most tragically, her children, and I didn't want to add to her pain with my own worries, which in any case were, at that point, just that: worries.

Immacuree and I had been through so much together! I thought back to when I met her with the other Tutsis in the corn field and how I had been shot and she had decided to run with me, to our time with Ingabire, to now, when with all we had been through, we vowed to stay friends forever and if we became separated to find each other after the massacre. I loved her, and she loved me. We exchanged information about where we were from and where and how we could find each other later. I told her that I might go back to Romania, to my grandmother, if I survived. Immacuree then said she wanted to ask me a question. "When I saw you for the first time," she said, "you looked like you didn't care if you were alive or dead. Why was that?" I then told her about my terrible upbringing, how my mother had abandoned me and my father and stepmother had abused me and told me I was better dead than alive and that if I were dead they would never have to be bothered by me. When she heard this, Immacuree could only look at me and cry. Composing herself, she said, "Christine, I am sure if your father is alive he is worried about you, and I am sure he regrets all the things he did to you."

I was polite to Immacuree, but I said, "I doubt he will ever regret anything he did to me, and that is why I don't want to talk about it." All I wanted, I said, was to survive, to find Chantal and to make contact with my family in Europe.

7

I COULDN'T UNDERSTAND HOW THE KILLERS COULD LAUGH AFTER SLAUGHTERING THE INNOCENTS

Immacuree and I started moving toward a low mountain, somewhere in the countryside outside of Kigali, which we thought would give us a safe place to hide if we could get to the top. There was a boarding school at the base of the mountain that we had heard the Hutu killers might decide to attack, which gave us even more reason to climb the mountain. In the end, though, it proved too difficult, so we decided to hide in some bushes near the school. It was quiet—we could even hear birds singing—and after all our turmoil, we liked having some peace for a while. Unfortunately, it wasn't to last, as, soon, we were startled by the sound of students screaming and men in uniforms with guns shouting—and shooting. It was the attack we had heard might happen. Since we'd been sleeping, we hadn't been aware of the militia arriving in their cars and trucks.

"What was that?" Immacuree said. Before long, we knew. We found out that the militia had yelled to the Tutsis to move to one side of a large room in the school and the Hutus to the other. The teachers said, please, they are children, and they are all Hutus. One of the men then hit the teacher in the face, and she fell to the floor screaming. The man said, "If you don't want to separate yourselves, you will all die. I will not ask you again." A boy said, "Please, sir, we are all sisters and brothers."

That was when the man gave the order to shoot, and the Interahamwe opened fire on all those innocent children and adults, not stopping until they thought there wasn't a living being left.

I couldn't take the screaming and covered my ears and closed my eyes. I was crying and shaking, and Immacuree held me tight while the killing was going on.

After they were done slaughtering everyone, the men left and ordered the younger Interahamwe to cut up the bodies to make sure no one survived. Immacuree and I had heard all that terrifying screaming and shooting, and then it was quiet, just as before. Only this time, we knew, it was the quiet of the dead.

I wanted to help in some way, but I thought that if I went into the school, I would find no survivors, only blood and dead people everywhere. At that moment, three girls and a teacher came out of the school. The girls were badly injured, and they and the teacher were covered in blood. Immacuree ran to offer aid, bringing them to where we had been hiding and helping them to the ground. They were hysterical, for themselves and for their friends.

One of the girls had lost a lot of blood and died before we could help her. The teacher and the other two girls were somehow able to get up and move on. As she was leaving, the teacher told us we must get away. She had heard the Interahamwe saying that they were coming back to search for more people to kill. So Immacuree and I once again found ourselves on the run.

It was the end of May, and here I was still running. One of my worst memories of that time was an especially gruesome roadblock. It had more dead people than any roadblock I had seen, with bodies piled up in a mountain of blood and death and limbs. The sight and smell were overwhelming. There was an especially notorious killer there who would demand money from his Tutsi and Hutu victims. First, pointing his gun, he would order them to sit in the street. Then he said he would spare them if they gave him money. But even if they paid, they would be killed. If the victims hesitated, the man would unpin a grenade and blow them to pieces.

The Hutu called Tutsis cockroaches and snakes. Many times they would kill by bashing in people's skulls. They said, "The way you kill a snake is by crushing its head."

God was constantly on my mind. I would pray but then lose faith. Why was God letting this happen? In the three months of the genocide, I said to God, you were nowhere to be found. Why did you let so many people die? So many woman and children? Such gruesome and unthinkable deaths? Why did you let other countries abandon us and not tell them to help? One time, I saw a man who was trapped at a roadblock talking to a man in a militia. He asked him how he could kill innocent people, saying, "What if the children being killed were yours?" The militia man said, "My children are not cockroaches. I'm just doing my job. The leaders say kill all the Tutsis; I kill all the Tutsis. There is no forgiveness." He said he was just there to obey. But why was God not "just there" *to help*?

When the militia man asked for the man's identity card, the man refused and said, "You can kill me if you want." So the militia man swung his machete and chopped the man's leg off, leaving him to die, screaming in pain, by the side of the road. "It is your fault," the man said. "No one messes with me." Then, as if the point needed to be made more emphatically, he viciously kicked the man in the back. A few minutes later, the militia man returned. Seeing that his victim was still alive, he shot him in the head. He had probably done him a favor.

To this day, I can't understand how during the genocide people could kill other people and laugh about it, something I saw over and over. Smiling, laughing men taking delight in slaughtering others. How could that be? It would take an army of psychiatrists to figure out, and even then, I don't think the answer would make sense.

As I continued to run and hide, the Interahamwe were not my only enemy. There was the problem of wild dogs that were eating the bodies decomposing in the cities and countryside. Sometimes, the dogs would try to attack and bite me, and I would have to scare them off with sticks or small stones. Either that or climb a tree as quickly as possible and hope I wouldn't be seen by my two-legged enemy.

You couldn't listen to RTLM without hearing people saying things like "the Tutsi are a dirty race. That is why we should exterminate them. We must get rid of them. This is the only solution for these Tutsi cockroaches." At that time, I didn't know very much about Hitler and the Nazis, even though my grandparents were Holocaust survivors, but people were saying the Hutu propaganda and killing were all-too-reminiscent of the Nazi's Final Solution. RTLM would follow their inflammations with songs saying "Let us rejoice, Hutu friends! Let us sing! All the cockroaches have been exterminated. We have worked hard to kill them so they will not come back to our country." Just as with the Nazis, it was propaganda with one goal in mind: to inspire and incite mass murder.

One time, when Immacuree and I were hiding, we witnessed an altercation that was among the most dreadful either of us had seen or would see. A man was pleading with a group of Interahamwe to let his friend go. One of the armed captors said, "Why should I? My job is to kill all the Tutsis." He told the man and the man's friend that he would not kill the friend with his gun because he didn't want to "waste" his bullets, which cost money. He walked over to the man to be killed and said, "Do you have any money? If you have money, I will shoot you with my gun. If you don't, I will use my machete." The man said he had 1,000 francs. The Hutu said, "My bullet is worth more than that," but he changed his mind and shot the man in the back of the head.

The other man started yelling and screaming. Beside himself with grief and panic, he cried out to his mortally wounded friend, "Please get up! Please don't die! I need you! Your family needs you! Please!" But his friend was dead, and the man was crying and couldn't stop.

Immacuree and I were in shock.

The Hutu who had just killed that innocent man then said to the man's friend, "Do you want to die too? If you don't leave, I will kill you also." Then the friend told the Hutu to put down his weapons and fight him hand to hand, which they then began doing. When the rest of the Hutu gang ran over to watch, they forgot about a group of Tutsi captives, so the captives ran away. Seeing this, Immacuree and I also ran, knowing the infuriated Hutus would stop at nothing to find their escaped hostages and others like us. We were right: when they realized what had happened, the Interahamwe started shooting into the bushes at anything that moved, but, thank God, the hostages and Immacuree and I escaped to freedom— for the time being, the two of us feared.

How I remember that day I ran to my friends Gerald and Nadine Nzeyimana's house, out of breath, knocking on the door, Gerald asking me what I needed and why I was there. I couldn't answer because I couldn't breathe and was just trying to get in the house and not even ask if I were welcomed and lock the doors behind me. Gerald asked me again what had happened, and I told him I didn't know if any of my family had survived and that there were fires everywhere. He asked if anyone had seen me coming into his house. I said no, it's dark outside, so I didn't think anyone had seen me. He hugged me and gave me something to eat and drink. Then Nadine started crying and hugging me and went to Brigitte's room to find a sweater for me and he asked me to get dressed. "We will hide you," she said, and led me to an outside storage shed filled with boxes and family possessions. She told me she would lock the door to the shed and said that if something went wrong, I could escape through a window in the back. I thanked her and took the blanket she offered. "Remember, God loves you," she said, and left.

The next day the killing started in their neighborhood and, along with it, the house searches. The Interahamwe barged into Gerald and Nadine's house and ransacked the premises, looking in all the rooms, including the storage shed, but they didn't find me.

I knew the Nzeyimanas were risking everything for hiding me, and I couldn't thank them enough. I spent another night at their house, and in middle of that second night I heard the sounds of people shouting and dogs barking. I found out the next day that machete-wielding Interahamwe had been erecting a checkpoint right behind the house and looking in the windows of people's homes. I thought that no matter where I hid, one day I would be found out and killed.

The next day Nadine and Gerald asked me to come into the house, and that was when I finally saw Brigitte. She was happy to see me and didn't even know I'd been hiding in her house till that moment! Later, Nadine said I could stay in the house, not the shed. "I feel bad that you had to stay there, Christine," she said, "but it was to protect you. I'm sure no one will show up to search the house again." I thanked her once more for helping me.

During my weeks on the run, as I was hiding and trying to stay alive, all I wanted was to find my family and see if they had survived. But I knew, just as Nyiradegeya and Fabrice had been killed, that my father, Valentine, my other stepbrothers and Chantal surely had also been taken from me. I could hardly bring myself to consider such a thought, but the alternative, that somehow, with all the carnage, they had survived, was just as unfathomable, although I clung to the hope because it was all I had. I prayed to God that they were alive, but I had only the faintest belief that God heard me. Maybe it was because I had had such a sad life. All through my 14 years, I thought, I'd never had a happy day, crying all the time, every day, it seemed, through the beatings, the criticism, the abuse, until, now, when the killings started, I almost couldn't cry anymore. It was as if my eyes—and my heart—had used up all the tears they had.

The Nzeyimanas were nice, and they tried to calm me down, but it was hard for me to relax. At bedtime, I was too scared to close my eyes. The night I stayed in the house, when Nadine showed me my bed, I told her I preferred to sleep underneath it because I was afraid of being discovered. And that is just what I did. Not only that: I slept with my clothes on. That way, I would be ready to race off if the house got searched in the middle of the night. Such was my existence during that time.

There were to be no house searches that night, and everyone slept, if sleep is what it could be called, without interruption. By morning, I was beginning to feel safer and had taken comfort in Nadine's comment the day before that the house wouldn't be searched again, even as I wondered how she could be so sure. Almost as soon as that thought had come into my head, everything went completely black. There was a loud knock at the front door, then a loud knock at the back door. Who would be knocking at both doors? We could hardly bring ourselves to ask. Gerald told Nadine, Brigitte, her older brother Johnathan, her younger brother Eric and me to hide. After a minute, he went to the front of the house. No sooner had he opened the door than a man raised his gun and shot him in the head at point-blank range. The man then entered the house, stepped over Gerald's body and found Nadine, trying frantically to find a place to hide, and shot her, too. He then found Johnathan and shot him dead, as well. Three shots, three executions.

Even though I had seen more people get killed than I could count, had almost become numb to it, still, I was in shock at this unbelievably cold-blooded carnage. I didn't have much time to dwell on it, though, as, from my hiding place under a couch, I smelled gasoline. My God, I said, they're going to set the house on fire!

Through the ensuing smoke and chaos, I somehow managed to escape with Eric and Brigitte, who, through her tears and fear, told me that the man who had killed her parents and brother had been a "friend" of her father's. Together, we shared the shock and horror at how friends and even family members had come to turn on one another, committing the ultimate crime against people they had loved, known, befriended, lived next to and even shared a bed with. Our young minds and battered hearts had no ability to comprehend such profanity.

We could hear the madness going on all around us. We found out later, for instance, that some neighbors of the Nzeyimanas had been attacked by other neighbors. The attackers had killed everyone in the house and then stolen their car and furnishings. There was literally no end to the depravity and slaughter.

At the arrival of darkness, Brigitte, Eric and I, frightened and feeling we didn't have a choice if we were to have any hope of surviving the killing in the immediate neighborhood, made the decision to walk to my aunt's house, about 10 kilometers (between six and seven miles) away. Our circumstances were dire: it was raining and cold, and we had neither food nor water to help keep us going. As I had been running for weeks and had "experience" in how to survive, I told everyone to stay together but that if one of us got caught, the others should run and keep running and not try to save the person in captivity. "Run for your lives," I told them, and meant it literally.

Progress was painfully slow because we had to be extra careful in our movements to avoid the killers, but also because we kept making time-consuming mistakes due to my unfamiliarity with the streets and neighborhoods we were walking in. As I looked at my watch and saw it was five o'clock, I realized that with daylight approaching we would have to get off the streets and find a place to hide. The sad reality, however, was that we knew no one in the area and had no place to go or hide. I tried to make Eric feel safe and protected as much as I could even though I was frightened and unhappy and didn't feel the least bit safe myself. But he was only seven and had just lost his parents and sister, so I felt that was the least I could do. I hoped he didn't sense that I, in my own state of dread, didn't believe a word I was saying.

There were no dry areas, so we were walking in muddy water, in what amounted to a bog. It didn't take long for trouble to develop. Tired, cold, wet and hungry and more or less oblivious to his surroundings, Eric suddenly found find himself sinking into the muddy sludge we had been trudging through. Soon, to everyone's dismay and alarm, he was stuck—and frightened. Brigitte tried to get him to calm down to keep us from being discovered by Hutus who might be nearby. In a few minutes' time, she and I found ourselves in the stinky mud, too, which made it harder to get to Eric. With Brigitte in more trouble than I, it fell to me to try to save the seven-year-old. But I couldn't swim and was worried that he and I might drown or get pulled under together. I thought back to when my cousin Damien drowned in a swimming pool when we were kids, and how I'd decided that day that I would never go into a swimming pool or near water again if I could help it.

After what seemed like forever, I was still struggling to get Eric out of the water and muck—first grabbing his hand and then putting him on my back, all the while watching for the snakes that seemed to be everywhere—but nothing worked; not only that, before long we started to get sucked in together. Eric was shrieking in fear and vomiting from the horrid stench, and I wasn't doing much better. I heard Brigitte scream, "Please hold on to him, Christine. Don't let him go." I realized I was Eric's only hope and told him and Brigitte I would do everything possible to get him out of there. But despite my efforts, the situation only got worse. Then, just when I was beginning to lose hope, a woman who had been hiding with her children and watching this all unfold rushed over and threw a pair of pants to me. With Eric on my back, and with me holding on to one pants leg and the woman the other, we were pulled out of the water and saved. The woman then rescued Brigitte, who had been in serious danger herself. If not for the help of this woman—a complete stranger—all of us almost certainly would have died. It was an act of kindness and courage that didn't happen often at that time, one that saved our lives, and we were extremely grateful to this very brave woman.

After rescuing us, she took Brigitte, Eric and me to her hiding place and told us that the Hutu regularly arrived with big trucks to dump bodies "from downtown" in that bog, which is why it smelled so bad. Those were rotting corpses that were making us sick! Hearing that almost made us sick all over again. The woman said she had taken her children to that spot because the Hutu, knowing the smell from the swamp was unbearable, had reasoned that no one would be able to hide there.

The woman, whose name we never learned, had two children, the oldest of whom was a girl about 11 and a boy about 8. She told us not to be scared when the trucks came. If we lay down and stayed still, she said, the Hutu wouldn't bother us. "Pretend you are dead," she said. Each night, she left her children alone while she went to her house nearby to cook food and bring it back to them. That particular night, she was also going to bring back a warm blanket for me and my friends. But she was late returning, and everyone, especially her children, was frightened that something bad had happened. As the oldest in the group, I told the children not to worry, but I had a feeling that something had gone wrong. Now her children were crying because their mother had never stayed away so long, and Brigitte and I had to hold the oldest girl down to keep her from going in search of the woman, saying there must be a plausible reason she hadn't come back yet and that she would return soon.

While all this was going on, we watched as the Hutu arrived in their trucks and dumped their victims in the bog. Sometimes one or more of the victims would not be dead but were severely injured and in bad shape and stacked among the slaughtered. You would see them moving, trying to get out from the mound of victims. It was too horrible to look at. Brigitte and I wanted to help, but we told ourselves these terrible sufferers wouldn't survive anyway, so we stayed with the children. I changed my mind later and went to try to help, but I was too hungry, tired and scared to do anything. We continued to wait for their mother all day the next day and into that night. Then that second night I heard someone in the bushes nearby running toward us. We all got scared but didn't move to keep from being seen. The person turned out to be the children's mother! We all broke down crying, and the woman apologized for frightening us but said when she got home all her neighbors had been killed and their houses burned down. "Our house was broken into and burglarized," she said. "They took everything, even the doors and windows and our animals and chickens." She said she heard a family screaming in terror as they were forced into their house by the Interahamwe then burned alive when the killers sent the house up in flames.

Still trembling, she said when the Interahamwe killed her neighbors, she threw all the food she had been cooking into a bag, put out the fire in her outdoor stove and hid in her back yard in a hole her husband had dug before the massacre began when Hutus had first started threatening Tutsis, because she knew the killers would come looking for her. Not finding her at the house is when they stripped it bare. "I don't care," this courageous woman said. "All I wanted was to get back to you, to make you safe." We said again how glad we were that she was back and had escaped the Hutu.

That night, another truck arrived with its cargo of bodies. As before, some of the "killed" were still alive. This time, instead of one or two, there were twenty or more! By the grace of God, we were able to pull all of them out of the pile and save their lives.

With the smell from the bodies becoming more and more unbearable and the Interahamwe now searching the area more thoroughly, the mother decided to take her children back to her house, or what was left of it, to hide in the hole her husband had dug in the garden. Hoping she would take us with her, we asked if we could hide there too, but she said there wasn't room and then left with her children, walking away without so much as a word of farewell. Brigitte said, "I can't believe she left us here and didn't ask us to go with her. She didn't even look back or say goodbye. I guess she doesn't care if we live or die." She, Eric and I were once again alone, without anyone to help us.

I made the mistake of bringing up the tragedy of, Nadine's and Gerald's deaths. Hearing about his family for the first time, Eric said, "You mean we will be alone, and I will never see my mother?" We will figure something out, Brigitte said to him, and he burst out crying, saying he was cold and hungry, he missed his parents and he wanted to go home to find his mother.

Brigitte tried to calm him down, but he kept crying, saying over and over, "All I want is my mother." It was heartbreaking. I told him his mother and father had gone to Heaven to be with God, and he got very quiet. But later, during the night, he started crying and screaming again, and Brigitte and I had to restrain him to keep him from running away to what we knew would be certain death.

By the next day, Eric had quieted down again. I guess he had come to accept the tragedy and reached some sort of understanding within himself about what had happened and its consequences for him. After spending those terrible days and nights with Eric, I came to really like and admire him and appreciate how well mannered, grown up, respectful, sweet and intelligent he was. It made it all the harder to consider the terrible tragedy that had befallen his family and him.

The situation grew more and more dangerous, so the three of us decided to move that night, the idea being to find my aunt's house once and for all. All the while, we were angry at that woman who'd left us alone, something we couldn't understand. We waited till night then walked till the sun came up and the Interahamwe were back in the streets. Luckily, we found a place to hide in a house that had a garden in the back with tomatoes, onions, bananas and, best for us, corn and tall beans that offered a perfect place to keep out of sight. In many parts of Africa then, people cooked outside in detached kitchens, especially if they were poor, as the owner of this house was. My friends and I hid in the garden at the house, making sure to be quiet and stay out of sight by day. We saw a lady come out of the house to gather and peel fruit and vegetables, but, since we didn't trust anyone, we couldn't risk telling her we were there. We watched her all day coming and going from the house until, finally, when she went in one more time, I took a plastic bag I had found and quickly tiptoed to her work area where I gathered up some of her food and ran back to our hiding spot, fortunately unseen by the woman. Soon she came back outside, but I assumed she didn't realize the food was gone because she never said anything or started looking for us. But thinking about it later, I decided she knew we were there but didn't speak up or call for help because she was probabably a nice lady.

In the streets, things were getting worse, with the fighting looking more and more like all-out civil war. There was shooting and bombing, and various armed groups were fighting one another. At night, the sky would be on fire from all the bombs and other explosives. it was impossible to know whether you were a target or whether the bullets and bombs were meant for others, so the only thing you could do was to stay hidden. Now we not only had to hide from the Interahamwe with their machetes; we had to hide from the military and other armed groups with their, what I found out later is called, "ordnance." It made the matter of survival that much more fragile and harrowing.

From our hiding place in the woman's yard, we could hear screaming and shooting coming from a nearby bridge. We found out later that Hutus were killing people and throwing them off the bridge—men, women and children. It was terrifying to hear the screaming and the guns and to know that there was no one there to help those poor people. At that moment, a man came running toward us covered in blood from a gunshot wound, crying that his wife and children had been killed on the bridge but that he had escaped, telling us we must find another place to hide because the Interahamwe had set up checkpoints everywhere and they were killing everybody, no questions asked. This man, who said his name was Fidel Rwemarika, looked at me and said with my light skin the Hutu would kill me on sight and that if I wanted to keep moving I needed something black to cover my skin, like shoe polish . . . or mud. With the ground still wet from rain, I took his advice and covered my face and arms with wet dirt.

All this time, the shooting and bombing were continuing, even worse than before, and people were screaming and dying. By now, the old lady knew we were in her yard, but she didn't want to scare us away. While we were still in hiding, one of the lady's sons and some of his friends arrived at her house. They were laughing about a family they had just killed, and one of the friends asked for some soap to wash their victims' blood off "before they ate." They were drunk—and all the more dangerous for it. "Let's eat and then go back to work," the son said. "We need to find the Tutsis and kill them all."

When the old lady harshly rebuked her son and his friends for killing innocent people—"someone God created," she said—he said to her, "Shut up. You are old and stupid. Don't you see that the Tutsis are responsible for the death of our president? We must kill every last one of them." Then he and his friends went inside the house to eat before returning to "work."

Fidel said he recognized one of the men as the person who had killed his family and shot him. He was crying even harder at seeing the killer again. He looked at the sky with anger and sorrow in his face. "I didn't do anything to keep them alive," he said. "I wish I were dead with them." We tried to help him, and he finally began to regain his composure. But he swore to get justice for his family. Then he told us again that we must leave —but without me! He said with my skin color I would bring attention to everybody, putting all in danger. "I will take your friends," he said to me. "If they stay with you, they will surely die." He said if Brigitte and Eric didn't want to leave with him that was fine and that he would go by himself.

I didn't want to lose Brigitte and Eric, and they wanted us all to stay together, too. But I also didn't want to put their lives in more danger by drawing increased attention to the four of us. We cried and hugged. I told them I loved them and said I would go to my aunt's house alone and that they should try to get there on their own. They said they weren't leaving me, but the more I thought about it, the more I thought Fidel was right. It was a hard decision, but I knew it was the safe thing to do. I made up a story, telling Brigitte I would leave and come back soon. I was too upset and just couldn't say goodbye, but I knew I had to do it to save and protect them. I told Fidel to make sure they were kept out of harm's way if I didn't come back. I gave Brigitte my watch and walked slowly away, saying that I was going to check the street to see if it were safe to leave. If I didn't return in 20 minutes, I told her, she and Eric and Fidel should set off without me. I hugged my friends again and said, remember, if I don't come back, go to my aunt's house. "She knows you and will protect you," I said. I looked at Fidel and knew that he saw right through my lies.

With tears in our eyes, we said our last goodbyes, and I walked off. I hadn't gone far when I saw a large group of MRND militia men with automatic weapons shooting into some bushes and trees. Realizing at once that I was in danger if I stayed on the ground, I decided to I climb a big tree, where I stayed until the militia men, who were focused on shooting at people on the ground, left later that night. As soon as it was safe, relatively speaking, to be on the streets, I climbed down from the tree and once again went in search of my aunt.

She lived on the other side of town in the country, in a town called Masoro, and my hope was that where she lived was safer than in the city. After walking all night and still not reaching her home, I stopped at a farmhouse, hoping to take refuge there. At once I saw two bodies on the ground and an infant next to them, alive and crying, left to die by the Hutu gangs. I grabbed the baby and ran to a corn field where I held her in my arms until she quieted down, and placing her on the ground, I went into the house to look for food. Finding none, I filled a jug with water and brought it back to my hiding place for the baby. After giving her some, I kissed her on the forehead and held her tight, telling her not to worry, that everything would be all right.

Looking around, I got the feeling that Masoro, a small town in the countryside near Kigali where most of the people were farmers and almost everyone knew one another, had been emptied of its people. I found out later that the Hutu had rounded up all the women and children and sent them to the elementary school for "safe keeping" and then had killed all the men kept behind on the spot. Assuming the two dead people were the baby's parents and that she was all alone, I decided I would keep her with me because otherwise she would certainly die. All the while, I had the feeling someone else was in the corn field, watching me. At that moment, a pregnant woman appeared with a two-year-old boy and came over to me. As she approached, I became frightened and worried. I told her to keep away, but she kept approaching, telling me to put the baby dawn. I refused, ready to run to save the child, when the woman, whose pain and fear I mistook for madness, told me that the baby I was holding was her niece, her dead sister and brother-in-law's daughter. "Her name is Angelique," she said. "I was watching you the whole time. I didn't know who you were, I'm nine months pregnant and I can't move that much." With tears in her eyes, she told me her name was Nina, that the baby's mother and father had been killed the day before and that she had been unable to rescue the baby because the Hutu had stayed at the house and were looking for her. Then she told me that she had been having contractions and that she was afraid if she didn't get help, she would die. But we both knew that if she tried to get help and were seen by the Hutu, she would be killed, and her son, too.

She said, "You are old enough to help me," and I told her that I would try, but we must move and find a safe place first. After a minute or two, she asked me where I was going. I told her to my aunt's house, which was not far away, and she asked me her name. I told her, and she didn't answer, but instead became very quiet and wouldn't say anything when I asked if she knew them or if something had happened to them.

"She is a good, caring woman and loves people," I said. "She'll help you with your baby." Nina became more and more visibly upset. "Christine," she said, "I am so sorry to tell you but they burned down your aunt's house, and I don't know if she and your uncle are alive or dead." I couldn't believe it. I didn't want to believe it. My beautiful, loving aunt and her wonderful husband, dead? Tell me it's not true, God! Then I remembered that I had told Brigitte to meet me there and became scared of what might happen to her, Eric and Fidel. I started crying for what possibly were more lost members of my family.

Nevertheless, Nina, her son, whose name was Sebring, a two-year-old, the baby and I set out for my aunt's house because I wanted to see for myself if Nina had been right about the fire. We walked for five minutes, and she started having pain. She said she couldn't go any farther and asked me to take the baby and her son and leave her there. I told her there was no way I was going to just leave her and her baby to die and that maybe we could find someone to help. I held her hand and said we needed to pray to God to keep us safe, and she looked at me and said God is nowhere to be found, he has abandoned us. But I told her she was lucky to be alive when so many had died and to please believe in God. We started praying and crying, asking God to help us.

Then Nina started having contractions and said the baby was coming, so I took off my t-shirt and put it on the ground to wrap the baby in when it came out. Poor Nina was lying on the ground, in pain but knowing she didn't dare scream, without water or medical care or anyone other than me, a 14-year-old girl who didn't know the first thing about delivering babies, to help. Then the baby's head started to appear and Nina was pushing to get it out. I told her she was doing a great job and to keep on pushing but she said she was too tired. I told her if she didn't push, then she and the baby would die, even though I didn't know what I was talking about. Through her tears and pain, she said, all right, Christine, I will try one more time, and I was praying and saying please, please, God, we need this baby and we need you to help. I was scared and all I did was to keep saying to God, where are you when we need you? You are the only doctor we have now. Then I gave up and sat next to Nina and started crying, getting sad and angry. I sat there and didn't know what to do or say, just quiet for a while crying and thinking that I would have to watch her and her baby die. Her son was only two years old and the other baby was so small, both sleeping in the grass, hungry. While I was thinking about how I could find food for them and Nina, Nina said, "Oh, God! I felt its head, Christine!"

When I asked her what she wanted me to do, she said I should pull the baby. "I'm scared," I said, but Nina helped give me confidence.

She said, "I'm going to push one more time, and I need you to pull him out." I grabbed the baby's head and did what Nina asked me to do. Then that baby started coming out, and before Nina or I knew what was happening, it was born right there in that corn field! I had delivered a baby girl! Nina was in a daze, happy to be the mother of a seemingly healthy daughter but too tired and grief stricken to enjoy the arrival of her new child to the fullest. I thanked God and covered the baby in my T-shirt and, once more, began to cry. For once, the tears were for the living.

As amazing as I had found the experience to be, there was little time to enjoy it because we were getting hungry. Over Nina's objections, and knowing it was risky, I announced that I was leaving to try to find food and water and that if something happened to me I would yell as loud as I could to give her warning. Nina told me to be careful and to return safely.

In just a few minutes' time, I found a garden behind someone's house and started digging and gathering up carrots and other vegetables and fruit and putting them in my T-shirt when an elderly woman appeared and walked in my direction. Seeing her, I became frightened and grabbed all my vegetables and started to run, but she told me not to worry, and I soon overcame most of my fear and realized with her friendly face and warm greeting that she was someone I could trust. Seeing that I was not wearing a top, that I was hungry and cold, that my shoes were old and ruined and hearing that I had three hungry friends, including an infant and a just-born baby waiting for me, she invited me into her house and cooked food for me to take back to Nina and her family.

The woman, whose name I would never learn, was in her 80s and said she was Tutsi. She told me how the Hutu had killed all her children and grandchildren and made her watch as they committed the horrible crimes. She was crying so hard that she could hardly tell me what had happened and said that she was hoping they would come back and kill her to put her out of her misery. Still in shock from what she had witnessed, she took me into her house where she showed me her family chopped into pieces like so many butchered animals. I couldn't believe what I was looking at. I was only 14 and seeing things that not even hardened military veterans or police see, and I was seeing them every day, every hour. It was making me sick. If possible, it seemed the killing was becoming more obscene and terrible. For no reason, I thought of my father and how, if I were to see him again, I would tell him I wasn't stupid after all, that I had survived because of my smart choices. It would be my chance to prove him wrong. But I wanted him to survive for more than that: I wanted him to survive because even though he mistreated me, I was still worried about him.

I had to get away from those butchered bodies and told the woman I needed to get back to my friends. For her part, she told me we all could stay with her, but I told her it was too dangerous and then, hugging and thanking her and telling I would never forget what she had done for me and my friends and again how sorry I was for what had happened, I left to find Nina and the others.

The next several hours may have been as harrowing as any I spent during the three months I was on the run. On the way back to Nina, I saw cars and trucks packed with Hutus returning to the village to finish the job of killing any Tutsis who might have survived the first massacre.

I knew if I didn't try to help her, the old woman would be killed by the returning gangs, so I went back to her house and convinced her to leave with me although I knew that wasn't something she wanted to do, even, or maybe especially, if it meant she might survive. As we walked, I had to harangue her to move faster or we both would be murdered by the returning marauders. And I knew that by standing around arguing about it, we were also putting Nina and her family's lives in danger. I told the woman there was a new mother and three babies who needed my help and that if she was going to waste time complaining about her physical condition and put everyone in danger, I would have to leave her. She continued to refuse to do anything I asked of her, so I made a very difficult decision: I left her behind.

Finally, after being away all afternoon, I returned to Nina and everyone. The most important thing was that none of us had got killed. But also important was that I had food and water for Nina and her family, especially the babies. Nina was happy to see me and asked me where I'd been so long, so I told her the terrible story about the woman but also about how generous and helpful she had been.

We continued to hear Hutus singing about killing Tutus and with the growing presence of the killers in the nearby streets, we talked about finding a safer hiding place. The newborn was tiny, weighing only five pounds. She came into the world screaming, happy and relieved, just as Nina and I were. We were always worried that the Hutus would hear the baby crying and come after us, but, thank God, that never happened. But it was so sad to watch a beautiful little baby born in such drama and turmoil, living in bushes with nowhere to go and no blanket or milk. Even when Nina tried breast feeding her, she continued to scream. Nina didn't want me to leave again, but I did, anyway, and went looking for a new place for us. I didn't get very far. I heard what sounded like a young woman screaming and realized she was being killed, so I became frightened and returned to our hiding place, where Nina and I decided to stay until dark. Then I began to worry about my elderly friend, not able to get her out of my mind. So I told Nina that was going back to try save her once more because she was old and Tutsi and didn't deserve to die at the hands of bloodthirsty killers.

I ran to her house, avoiding the Hutu in the area, and told her that she was going with me and that I wouldn't take no for an answer, saying I wouldn't leave without her. I told her I would drag her with me if I needed to. If she wanted to go back after a few days, I told her, she could because by then the Hutu would have killed all the Tutsi and would have no reason to still be in her neighborhood. We left and had only been gone a little while when we heard voices and so hid in some bushes within view of her house. That was when we saw the Hutu approach it and set it on fire. Sickened, we could only watch as it burned to the ground. The Tutsi had probably hoped the woman was trapped inside, burning along with the building.

Even though she was crying over what she had just witnessed, she thanked me for getting her out of the house in time. "I wasn't going to leave you there," I said. "I left you before because all you were doing was complaining and putting everyone in danger." Now, I told her, she would have to keep up, or we would both be facing a death sentence.

In addition to her and Nina and her family, I was also worried about Nadine and Eric and that man Fidel, whom I'd told to go to my aunt's, and Immacuree, who had saved my life. I felt responsible for their survival, even if I also felt helpless to do anything about it.

Eventually, the woman and I made it back to Nina. Soon we heard Hutus nearby, and Nina begged me to take her children and run, saying she knew she wasn't in any condition to keep up and adding that her newborn needed milk, which Nina was unable to give her. I didn't want to leave her and my elderly friend behind, but I knew the most important thing was to save the children, so I put the baby on my back, took Sebring by the hand and cradled the newborn in my arms and started to leave. But before we could get away, the Hutus found all of us. Smiling and saying, look, we have more women, they dragged us to a nearby house used to imprison captured women and girls. It was crowded, everyone there was naked, and every day the Hutus would pick some out and rape them and then kill them behind the house.

With Nina sick and the newborn in need of medical attention, we were worried about what would happen, terrified that we would be raped and killed. We knew that even children and babies were being killed: the Hutu understood that if they killed the parents, the babies and young children would die anyway from starvation or wild dogs, which would eat them alive.

Right away, I saw Brigitte and Eric, who had been captured the previous day. It made me so happy to see them alive; it was a miracle . When I asked Brigitte about Fidel, she said he had been killed by one of the men in the school and that that same man had raped her. She was crying and showed me the bruises on her face and hands, and I hugged and tried to comfort her, but it the reality was that we seemed to have no hope of survival as we were captives of men who had sworn our people's annihilation. I told Brigitte that she could help me with the babies and that we would figure out a way to escape, maybe that night. Nina wanted us to go without her, saying she was sick and would die anyway, but Brigitte and I said we weren't going to leave her behind, that we were all together and that the children needed her. We had all been through hell together, and we had all become close and truly loved one another. Right then, the Interahamwe ordered everyone to sit down. They then went around the room with their bloody machetes looking for people to kill. They came over to where we were sitting, and we began shaking and becoming cold with fear that one or more of us would be chosen. After looking at everyone, they didn't choose Brigitte or me; they chose the old woman and Nina, the mother of the two babies. I was terrified for them, but at the same time I looked down trying to hide behind a woman who was sitting in front of me. Right then, I broke down crying, seeing again the brutality and heartlessness of these murderers of helpless, innocent people.

We were all crying as Nina, screaming, cried out, "Please take care of my children," but I looked away because I didn't want the Hutu to know I was with her. I felt terrible, but I knew, as did Nina, that if we acknowledged her, we would be the next to die. Then the woman, who remained anonymous, said, "Thank you, my child. Don't give up, and remember, you are too young to die." Feeling like a traitor, I ignored her just as I had Nina, looking down and refusing to make eye contact with her or with the militia men. As my friend were being taken away, one of the Hutu kicked Nina hard in the back, adding a painful, cruel indignity to what was about to be her last moment of life. How I wished I could do something to save their lives. Within minutes, an armed Hutu angrily asked whom our friends had been talking to, but he never got an answer.

My worries and fears then turned to how I was going to get out of that horrible place with those babies and my friends. That evening many of the Interahamwe left the house, so there were only a few of them to watch us for the night. They moved everyone to the back yard and told us to stay there and not to move and that we were to sleep on the ground. They had machetes but no guns or rifles. Therefore, my friends and I thought this might be our chance to escape. As we were talking, a women sitting behind was crying for her daughter, who had been taken that day. The woman didn't know what had happened to the girl, so she got up and shouted that she didn't care if she were killed; she was going to find her daughter no matter what. She walked over to some Hutu and said something to them we couldn't hear, but it clearly angered them. One of them got up from his chair and left. When he came back, he had the head of the woman's daughter in his hand and gave it to her, saying take it and go sit down and be quiet. The woman began screaming hysterically and calling him every name she could think of. Making the tragedy even more depraved was that the Hutu enjoyed her insults and her suffering. Then one of his henchmen yelled at the poor woman to "shut up," saying, "I didn't ask you to be a Tutsi." He told her that all the women and girls would be killed in the morning and asked if she wanted him to kill her now. She said they had killed all her family, so they would be doing her a favor if they killed her, too. With that, the Interahamwe spit in her face, pushed her to the ground and kicked her in her side. But he didn't kill her, wanting to prolong her suffering as long as he could.

That evening they gave some of us rice to eat, but I didn't get any. Why were they feeding us if we were going to be killed the next day?

It didn't make sense. But then nothing made sense, and that was the least of it.

Soon, twenty Hutus showed up with machetes, grabbed some women and took them and killed them. But one woman didn't die. Her legs dangled and she had an open wound in her forehead. In shock, she was unable to speak. Someone had found her lying with the dead. Her name was Epiphany, and I knew her from Remera, the town where I lived growing up. She had lost her husband and all five of her children, but the Interahamwe had brought her to the house just like everyone else because to them there was no such thing as too much suffering.

8

CHEATING DEATH: ANGELIQUE AND I SURVIVE

Brigitte, Immacuree and I came up with a plan of escape. Brigitte would take the newborn, Immacuree would take Sebring, and I would take Angelique, and we would all run in different directions. We waited till the Hutu were asleep or drunk, then Immacuree climbed the fence that surrounded that place of horror, and after I handed Sebring to her, she took off running , unseen by the Hutu guards. Then Brigitte and Eric, carrying the newborn, took off in a different direction, also unseen by the Hutu. Finally, it was Angelique's and my turn. I climbed the fence holding tight to her, and when I came down on the other side, ran as fast as my tired legs and worn-out shoes would carry me. Although I couldn't find Immacuree and Sebring, it wasn't long before I discovered Brigitte, Eric and the newborn hiding in a nearby field. We decided to keep moving even though we didn't have a destination. Some people said everyone was going to the Hotel Mille Collines, but I wasn't sure we would be safe.

At least I had Angelique, who was cute and lovable, in my arms. I would talk to her and tell her everything was going to be fine, reminding myself I had to be strong for her. But there was no food or water, and I became worried for her wellbeing. Also worrisome were my wounds from before, which were itchy, bloody and infected from all the dirt and unhealthy surroundings I had been in. With no doctors or other medical care available, I began to fear that my chances of dying from an illness were even greater than from being killed by the Hutu.

There was so much fear and paranoia everywhere that no one was willing to come to the aid anyone else, with friends and even family refusing desperate calls for help, so I knew that it was useless to ask. With their mass killings, the murderous Interahamwe had delivered an unambiguous message to the populous: reach out to others and you will die. More horrible, even, than that was that some of those very killers had been your friends and neighbors for years. You would see your best friend with a bloody machete looking for you, wanting to destroy you and your family. People you thought who loved you and cared for you are now robbing you and desperate to kill you. Your husband is killing women, children and babies. These men woke up with one thing on their mind: killing as many unarmed, innocent people as possible. Their wives were powerless to stop them. Clearly, and tragically, the paranoia and fear were more than warranted.

I held Angelique close and tried to comfort her and keep her warm and cried every day because she didn't have anything to eat. I tried to think and prayed to God otherwise, but if I were honest with myself, I knew there was little hope for this baby the angels had sent me named Angelique.

With my friends, I kept running, hoping to keep away from the Interahamwe and, somehow, to stay alive. My luck wasn't always good, as when I found myself standing next to a Hutu who was a leader of a militia and was making fun of some Tutsi women. I was standing there, holding Angelique to my chest, when he called me forward and started asking me questions, like what was my name and why was I so dirty. I didn't want to make eye contact with him, but he ordered me to look him in the eye, and it was then that I saw what evil looked like.

He started hitting me and asked me if the baby was mine. When I told him she was my little sister, he smacked me in the face and said, "People who lie to me die. I am going to ask you one more time. Where did you get that baby?" Now Angelique was crying, and I knew I was in trouble and became frightened that he would take her from me. When he asked me to put her down, I refused, and he hit me again and I lost control of my bladder. He grabbed Angelique and threw her on the ground. She started crying even harder; I wanted to pick her up, but the militia man wouldn't let me, threatening to kill her if I didn't tell him where I got her. He asked me how old I was, and when I told him, he hit me again, but I didn't care; all I wanted was to get away with Angelique. I bent down to pick her up and one of the Hutu started laughing, saying she wet her paints and mocking and making fun of me. The Interahamwe leader told one of the men to get a bucket of water for me to shower with then they made circle around me they asked me to get naked. I refused, so one of them grabbed Angelique from me and said now take your clothes off. I did what they asked. Then one of them said to the others, "That's enough. She doesn't have breasts and is too young for me to look at. She, she reminds me of my daughter." I took a shower in front of all those Interahamwe and didn't care if I was naked, in fact feeling lucky that no one touched me. [Did the girl get to put her clothes back on?] Then the leader with the evil-looking eyes came back with a beer, which he ordered me to drink. When I said I didn't, he said, "I will count to twenty. I want you to drink this beer as fast as you can." I started drinking and finished the bottle as I was told. I begged them to let me go when the leader said, "Oh, did we ask you our favorite question, the one we ask everyone?" He laughed a wicked laugh. "Are you Hutu or are you Tutsi?"

When I heard that, I knew I would have to lie to have any chance of saving the baby and myself. "I am Hutu," I said. The man came closer to me and said, "You are a liar." Beating me on the head, he said,

"Do you think I am stupid? Her skin is darker than yours." He started sharpening his machete and circling me, saying, "Do you know we kill Tutsis? And this is Hutu land?"

I just sat there, hoping and praying for Angelique's and my lives. They kept hitting me and making fun of me and said they would kill me in the morning. I tried to put up a brave front, but all I could do was cry.

For some reason—I told myself it was because God was looking down—Angelique and I weren't killed although that was far from the end of our misery. The next day, the Interahamwe led a group of naked women and children to a bridge, where they told us they were going to kill everyone because they didn't know what else to do with us. As we approached the bridge, I looked down and saw thousands of dead bodies and blood everywhere, with human heads, legs and arms strewn about like broken furniture. Then I heard a woman in front of me scream and say, "Oh, God! He just killed her and pushed her off the bridge! We are all going to die!" She started panicking and crying saying she didn't care anymore, that she had been raped and her family killed. "I am already dead, anyway," she said, and started laughing at the Hutu. When one of them, carrying a machete and a gun, went over to her, she said she wanted to die, and he brought over another man and said, "We have a problem here. This whore wants us to kill her." The other man laughed and said, "Then let her go. She will die by someone else's hand." We could not believe they were letting her go. Everyone on that bridge wanted to run, and here was someone who could but wouldn't. I said to her, "You are lucky. Please, go." The Interahamwe, shoving and pushing, kept us moving, so I never did find out what happened to that woman, but I hoped she got away and survived.

Crying, I held Angelique tighter and tighter and whispered to her that I was sorry I couldn't protect her. She looked at me and smiled and touched my face. It was as if she were telling me goodbye. I looked into her eyes and at her beautiful smile and knew that was the last time I was going to see her. "I love you, Angelique," I said. "May God watch over you."

I wanted to run but even though I wasn't superstitious I wondered if all my lucky days of escaping death had been used up, even as, looking in front of me, I could see it was a matter of minutes and 10 women in front of me before I was going to die, and Angelique with me. The terrible reality was that we were already on the bridge. My choices were to jump off or try to run through the mob of killers to freedom. Now there were only three women ahead of me. I was standing in blood. Only two women left. Panic stricken, I pushed the woman behind me aside and ran for my life, and Angelique's. Then I heard shots and felt fire in my body. I fell to the ground, shot in the back of my leg.

Bleeding profusely, I was dragged by the Interahamwe back to the bridge where I was beaten and told I would be killed and thrown down to join the countless other dead below. For the Interahamwe, there was no wasting their time checking your papers to see whether you were Tutsi or Hutu or looking at your nose or your feet or seeing if you were tall and beautiful. They just killed everyone and threw them to the hellish place below.

I remember seeing Angelique flying. I screamed and saw a machete coming toward my head. I remember seeing other dead people on the bottom of the bridge. I don't remember how I got there, but I must have been thrown off the bridge like Angelique and everybody else. I lay with all those bodies for a long time, and at first I had the sensation of being dead, myself. Where was my darling Angelique? Was she still alive? I remember a dripping on my face and thought it must be raining. I also heard voices of people who were searching among all the bodies, many bloated and putrefied, saying "We found one who is still alive. Come and carry her. Put her on your shoulders." To me, it was as a dream, a waking nightmare, and I wasn't sure I hadn't made those voices up. I felt someone pulling me and trying to clean my face, which was covered with blood, with the skin of my face torn open by the machete's cuts. Someone asked me my name. I could hear the shooting and screaming, and I thought he was there to kill me. "I'm a good guy," he said. "I'm here to help you." I don't know why, but I believed him. The man cleaned my face, which was sticky with blood. He asked me if I was hungry, but instead I kept asking for Angelique. "A baby," I said. "A baby."

I found out later the man was with the patriotic front, and he told one of the other rebels I was asking about a baby but that he didn't know if maybe I was delirious or in shock. Through my pain and disorientation—I hardly even knew my own name—I told the other rebel about Angelique, but when they looked they couldn't find her. Then the fighting started again, and the rebels and the Hutu were shooting at each other. I couldn't get up because my wounds were too painful. I had broken legs from being shot and cuts on my head from the machete, and everything was terrible, when a rebel picked me up and threw me over his shoulders. Shooting and running, he carried me back to the rebel base and cleaned my wounds.

There were no doctors or nurses there. The man told me he was going to remove the bullets from my legs with a knife. With no medicine of any kind, he gave me something to bite on and told me not to scream because he didn't want the Hutus to know where he and his comrades were. "I will count to five," he said, "and then get the bullets out." The other soldiers held me down, telling me I was lucky to be alive and that I was strong and brave and please not to yell. One rebel cleaned my face while another removed the bullets. The pain was excruciating, and I begged them to stop. But they said if they didn't do this, I would die from infection and told me they didn't have time to deal with my complaining, that there were too many others who needed help. They told me they weren't leaving me till the work was done and held me down and did it. Then, when they put whiskey on my wounds, it was all I could do to keep from screaming again. One of the men told me to close my eyes and said, "God be with you. I hope you believe in him." I said, "Yes, I do," and he smiled, saying he and the others were there to help and protect everyone and that I didn't have to worry anymore.

But worry was all I did because I wanted to find Angelique. I told them that I knew she hadn't died and that we had to go back and find her. "Please, I beg you," I said. "I'm sure she is still alive." But they said they had found no baby alive and that they had found me and three other women survivors but that everyone else at the bottom of the bridge was dead. So they wouldn't go back and look. Besides, they said, they would get ambushed by the Interahamwe if they did. I started crying for Angelique and said I would go find her myself if I could walk. They wanted to know my name and where I was from, but I couldn't remember anything and, anyway, all I could think about was baby Angelique and what she was wearing and how small and vulnerable she was. But I couldn't move and was very sick and in bad shape, so I had no choice but just to lie there. And pray for Angelique.

One day about a week later when I was still in the "recovery area" with other survivors and feeling sadder than ever about Angelique, I heard the sound of a baby crying. I was immediately overcome with emotion, hoping against all hope and praying to God that it might be Angelique. "Oh, God, that is Angelique! That is my Angelique!" I said. I called one of the soldiers and asked him to see if the baby had on red pants and black socks. He told me to try to calm down, that he would find out. In a few minutes, he came back and said a woman with the baby said it wasn't hers and that she had found it last week at the bottom of the bridge. The soldier told her there was someone who wanted to see her, so the woman came over and brought the baby. It was Angelique! I starting crying harder than I'd ever cried. I thanked the woman over and over for being such a good person. She looked at me and said, "I hope you will keep her and look after her. I lost all my children and she was all I had." Then the soldier told me that Angelique had suffered a broken leg and rib but that she would be all right. He told the woman that my injuries, on the other hand, were very serious and that I might not live. Knowing this, and what she had lost, I told the woman, whose name I wouldn't learn till later, that she could keep Angelique, but only on one condition. She asked what the condition was. I told her it was that I could visit her any time I wanted. She smiled at me and said, "Yes." And then she said, "Thank you."

Everywhere, the UN forces were helpless, unwilling or unable to do anything to stop the slaughter. Before that unspeakable time on the bridge, there was an incident when I was being chased by some Hutu, saying, there is a white girl, shoot her, but I outran them. Then a UN truck appeared with peacekeepers from Belgium. I screamed to them for help, and they said they weren't allowed to help us, but they weren't lucky, either, as the Hutu executed them right there. With the killings, the Hutu wanted to force the U.N. out of Rwanda, and in this mission they succeeded.

Weeks later—it was early or mid-June—even though there was no access to news, rumors were circulating that the Rwandan Patriotic Front was fighting back against the Hutus, with help from Tutsi survivors of the genocide and refugees from Burundi and other countries, and that some progress against the *genocidaires* was being made—too late, it would turn out, to save the lives of up to a million Rwandans and the displacement of two million more as refugees.

9

MY FAMILY'S FEARS AND FLIGHT
DURING THE MASSACRE

During the three months I spent running and hiding, and knowing the horrible deaths suffered by thousands upon thousands of Rwandans, I was terrified about what might have happened to my family, especially Chantal. Had they lived? Were they safe? Had they been killed like so many others? As with many survivors of war throughout history, my family's and my experience with the trauma of the genocide made it extremely difficult and in some cases impossible to talk about what we had witnessed and suffered, which is why it wasn't till years later that I learned how Chantal and others of my family had managed to survive.

My father, Valentine and their surviving children had been taken hostage by the Interahamwe, without even having a chance to cover the bodies of my grandmother and s murdered in their house. There followed a shootout, with some of the Interahamwe killed by Tutu rebels, allowing my father and everyone to escape. Often going without food and water, they spent the next several days making their way to a village close to where my grandmother had lived on a farm she owned with lots of cows and goats.

Most of the people in the village were Hutu, one of whom my

father knew and trusted. This man offered to let my father and the others stay in his guesthouse, saying that everyone would be safe. That night there began a strange, fearful game of people making threats and then receiving threats to ward off the first threats, with the threats escalating in ferocity and no one being completely sure if his side was safe. It started with a woman friend of my father's host telling my father that she had heard that Hutu friends of the host were planning to come to the guesthouse and kill my father and everyone else. When my father asked his friend about this, he assured my father that nothing would happen, and that anyone who did threaten my father would have to answer for it with the host. To show his sincerity, he then fed my family a traditional Rwandan meal.

Later that night, someone pounded on the door of my father's quarters, saying, "Open up, Leonard." My father's friend, who was in the guesthouse with my family at the time, told my father not to open the door, that if he did, the man would kill everyone. Then the man at the door said if the door wasn't opened, he and his friends would burn down the house.

The threats continued, with my father's friend telling the man that if he so much as touched his house, he would kill him and his friends, too. Hearing that, the man said he would get more reinforcements and kill not only the host but "the Tutsi friends you are trying to hide and protect." Then, it was my father's friend's turn again; he told the Hutu, "Do what you want. But I will tell everyone that you are married to a Tutsi. That means they will kill your wife and your children, too. And after they kill them, they will kill you."

That was the last of the threats, or so everyone thought, as the Hutu got worried that his friends would find out about his wife and left. But the ordeal wasn't over for my father, Valentine and the others: My father's friend said he and everyone should leave the house "in case they come back." He took them to the Nyabarongo, a major river in Rwanda, gave them a small boat and told them to be careful crossing because there were Hutu all around and they would try to drown them. To make matters even more perilous, the river, the largest dumping ground for the dead anywhere, was clogged with the bodies of thousands of people killed in the genocide and was infested with crocodiles, alligators and snakes.

It turned out the would-be killer of my family returned to the house with other Hutus, intending to kill everyone, but by then my father, Valentine and the boys were in the river, and my father's friend had gone into hiding, so this was one time the Hutu were not able to carry out their butchery.

By now, the Tutsi rebels were making headway against the government, but the Hutu were not about to be defeated without taking as many innocent Tutsis and Hutus with them as possible. Especially disposed to buy into the government propaganda were the uneducated Hutu. They were overwhelmingly the ones who did the killing, to, as they were told, "fight for Rwanda," to leave nothing behind, even more so now that the government was sensing it would be forced from power, and probably soon.

As everyone now knows, up to a million Rwandans lost their lives because the world did nothing. I had friends who died in Kicukiro, a suburb of Kigali, when they and thousands of others were left helpless and unprotected by UN peacekeepers. Speaking in Kicukiro in 2009, on the seventh anniversary of the start of the genocide, President Kagame said of the international community, "Of course . . . the guilt is indeed how the people of Rwanda were abandoned at their time of need by people who were here supposedly to protect them." The U.S. and other countries evacuated their own citizens and other favored groups but did nothing for the Rwandan people. Because of this, by July, when the bloodletting had at last come to an end, Rwanda was a decimated, destroyed country. You would walk or drive for miles and see nothing but bodies and burned homes, or the doors and windows of the few houses still intact open to the elements, with only dogs on streets. Rwanda was quiet, in the way that death is quiet.

It would be impossible for anyone who didn't experience the genocide first hand to comprehend the pain my fellow survivors and I were feeling–our agony and our tears. As a survivor of this evil, I knew my life would never be the same, just as the lives of my fellow survivors would never be the same. The million dead in that hundred-day spasm of bloodletting, out of a population of seven million, was one of the worst slaughters in human history, and with two million more made homeless together with those who fled the country, there were few if any Rwandans who weren't affected by the genocide. Even now, 20 years later, the wounds aren't close to healing.

Paddling the boat with their hands, my father, Valentine and the boys made it to the other side of the Nyabarongo, but that didn't mean they were safe. Far from it. They had to run a gantlet of Interahamwe garrisoned in a village called Rwankuba, where they were all threatened with death. A man there who knew my father told him he had been present when I was shot and thrown over the bridge to my presumed death. The man who told my father this, a Hutu, knew him from when my father was a boy on my grandparents' farm. The man walked over to some of his friends and said, "Do you see that man over there? He is Tutsi and his daughter got killed by my friends three weeks ago." He then returned to my father and said, "I saw your daughter get killed. Oh, man, that girl was a fighter. She tried to run—she was fast, too, so we had to shoot her in the legs to get her to stop—but she is dead now." Then he and his friends started laughing, taunting my father and making fun of me.

My father, Valentine and their children were running all the time. During one of their attempts to elude the Hutu, they suddenly realized that Adrien had been left behind. Valentine told my father to go back to look for him, but he refused because he knew if he went back he would be killed. He told Valentine they had to keep moving, but she started crying, saying they had already lost three children—Chantal, Fabrice and me—and said she was going back to find him.

The area she looked in had been the scene of deadly fighting between the RPF and Hutu government forces and was now mostly controlled by the rebels. Valentine kept calling Adrien's name and eventually he heard her and called back. He had become frightened by all the shooting and had hidden behind a tree and was, almost unbelievably, not only alive but unhurt. However, as Valentine was running to him, she was shot in the back and, losing blood, fell on top of him. While my father was being selfish and cowardly, Valentine had put her life at risk to protect her son. Fortunately, Valentine and Adrien were rescued by the RPF, and it turned out her wound was not serious.

It may seem irrational to use the word lucky to describe anything having to do with the genocide. But, looking back, that is how I felt at the time, at least in some respects. Chantal, as I found out later, was lucky to have escaped a mass killing at her school and find refuge in the Congo. My father was lucky to have escaped being killed when everyone else in his village had suffered such a fate. Valentine and the rest of her children were lucky to have escaped almost certain death. Baby Angelique was, I hoped, in safe and loving hands with the woman from the camp. And I was lucky to have avoided being killed and raped during the three months I spent trying to survive.

Even though I felt "lucky," the fact was that I was still very sick. Thanks to the RPF, I was transported to a hospital, King Faisal, in Kigali, where I spent many months in treatment for my wounds and infections. During this time, I thought and dreamed endlessly about the war and about my family, especially Chantal, and recalled how the two of us had been through so much, how much we loved each other, how she was my only friend and how we suffered all our lives together. I cried for her every day, praying she was all right. And I cried for myself, fearing what my life would be like if she were not.

As would be expected in the poor, war-ravaged (and abandoned) country that Rwanda was at that time, medical care, even in hospitals, was minimal. And no matter how dedicated the doctors and nurses were, the reality was that palliatives and other medicine were almost completely non-existent, and food and water were available only intermittently, if at all. Then there was the sad, ceaseless din of people in pain, often from horrifying injuries, crying for loved ones and for help. I was no different. I had no feeling in my legs, and the wounds on my head were open, infected and untreated. All those months surviving the genocide and now the doctors were in effect telling me I would die of my injuries because there was no medicine to treat them. To have fought so hard and dodged death so many times only to lose my life that way—especially now that it looked as if the genocide were coming to an end—seemed a bitter mockery.

10

MY LIFE AND NIGHTMARE AFTER THE WAR: A FALSE RECOVERY

It was mid-July, and finally the RPF had gained control of the country. *The genocide was over.* One hundred days. One million dead. Two million homeless and stateless. As help arrived, Rwanda began its long journey out of hell. At King Faisal, there were thousands of victims, many of whom, despite receiving improved care, would not survive their wounds. Those who didn't were taken to a building in back of the hospital and their bodies burned.

When the RPF assumed power, over a million Hutu, fearing reprisals and revenge, fled to the Congo (then called Zaire) and other countries, such that by this time, Rwanda, counting the dead and the refugees, both Hutu and Tutsi, had lost an almost unimaginable 30 percent of its population.

The new government, under President Kagame, worked to rebuild the country, figuratively and literally, offering new homes to those who had become homeless and a National Unity and Reconciliation Commission (NURC) to help promote cooperation and cohabitation among traumatized people and communities. Also, local trials, called *gacacas,* were employed to try the thousands of people accused of having taken part in the massacres and to bring justice to their victims.

With Valentine having survived her wounds, she and my father and their children returned to Kigali. They buried my grandmother and brother and other family members who had died and then tried to rebuild their lives, starting with their home, which had been destroyed down to its walls. They assumed I was dead and tried to find my body, but they didn't find me, dead or alive, for months. To their relief and happiness, they learned that Chantal had survived and soon would be coming home, albeit to a different house and household, but they, in particular Chantal, were distraught to have lost me.

Time went by and everyone gradually gave up looking for me, even as I lay in the hospital with no one knowing who I was because I had refused to give out my name—or hardly to talk at all. The nurses called me Muzungu ("white") and that was my name during my nearly seven months of recuperation.

One day the nurses wheeled me into a waiting room crowded with other patients when a woman who had known me from church started screaming and yelling to her friend Beatrice. "Oh, my God, it's Christine! She's alive!" She ran to me and hugged me, and we both started crying, but I didn't say anything to her. She told the nurse everyone had been looking for me or, more accurately, for my body for months but had given up. Then the nurse asked the woman my name, and she told her. Because there were no phones and no one had any money for cars, Beatrice walked to my father's house to tell him about me while the woman who recognized me, Uwimana, spent the rest of the day in my room, asking questions. But I didn't talk to her; I couldn't remember anything or anyone except two people: Chantal and baby Angelique. Uwimana asked a nurse what was going on with me, why I wasn't talking. "Is she angry"? she said. The nurse told her I had been mostly mute since the day I was brought there by soldiers six months before and had been in and out of a coma as well. She said the doctors thought I'd lost my memory from head injuries I had suffered.

When my father and Valentine heard I was alive, they ran to the hospital to find me. But at first I didn't—or maybe didn't want to—recognize them. It was only a few days later that all the terrible memories came back, and I remembered how much I hated them. But my father hugged me and told me that he missed me and he loved me. Best of all, he shared the wonderful news that Chantal had survived! He then asked me to forgive him and for the first time in his life showed that he cared. Also for the first time in his life I saw him cry. Valentine kissed me and hugged me and started crying, too, and offered thanks to God.

Then my father brought up the past. "Please, Christine," he said. "I know you are angry, and you and I have never been close. I am so sorry. Please, my child, forgive me. Please talk to me. I am glad you are alive, and I would do anything for you to forgive me for all the pain I caused you. I need you to give me a chance to be a good father to you." He was holding my hand and crying. But the only thing in my mind was that my sister, my best and only friend, my indispensable Chantal, was alive.

The doctors told my father about my wounds and said I wasn't ready to be discharged. When my father was sharing this information with Valentine, a nurse came into the room and said, "Is Muzungu talking now?" My father said my name was Marie-Christine, that I went by Christine and that I wasn't talking because I was angry with him. Hearing this, the nurse said, "No, your daughter has hardly spoken since she was brought here because she is sick and was so traumatized by the war."

That night the anonymous woman I shared my room with died of her infections, and I thought I would be next because I had the same problem. As I watched the hospital workers take her away, I thought about how she had never had a single visitor that I knew of in all the months we had shared our room. She had said that her husband and all her family had been executed by the Hutu. So she died alone and sad. It was heartbreaking and a terrible reminder that among the genocide's victims were its survivors.

Valentine, after seeing that my roommate had died and knowing I was angry, took my hand. "Christine," she said, "you are a child of God, and you are alive. Your father and I prayed for you all this time. We thought you were dead, and we wanted your forgiveness in heaven.

Now God has given us a chance to see you alive. We are so grateful." She was crying. "Can you please talk to me? Or just shake your head or move your eyes if you can hear me?" She said that Chantal had always "known" that I was alive and that someday I would walk in the door. Valentine then started praying for me, and I remember her saying, "God, I know you can hear our prayers. I trust you that Christine will get better and we will take her home." She said, "Help her, God. She needs you." At that, I opened my eyes and said, "Amen!" as loud as my weakened state would permit, and Valentine said, "Christine, did you just speak? Please, Christine, talk to me." I didn't know what to say, so I said nothing, something I chose to do to the people who had betrayed me in the past. Valentine started crying and said that she guessed hearing me was an illusion. "I thought I heard your voice," she said, disconsolately.

The next morning was the day I had been waiting for for months and months: Chantal was coming! I told myself if I remained mute around others, I would speak, and speak with all the pent-up emotion I'd been holding in all this time, with Chantal. When she walked into my room, all I wanted to do was get up and throw my arms around her, but the reality was I couldn't move. Even if I could, she would have beaten me to it, as she ran over and hugged me and wouldn't let go. Through our sobbing, we said how much we loved each other, how we couldn't believe this was actually happening and how happy we were finally to be reunited. It seemed as though we held onto each other for hours.

Chantal related how our father had said to her the previous night that I hadn't wanted to talk to him, but she told me he had changed. "All the time you were missing," she said, "he was nice and was always asking me to forgive him for all the pain he had caused you and me growing up." I was astonished at these words from Chantal. She then said, "He was in agony about losing you and what he had done to you and said that if only he could see you he would tell you how sorry he was and ask for your forgiveness." I was lying there fighting for my life, and the truth was I didn't care about him or what he wanted from me, so I looked at Chantal and shook my head and rolled my eyes. I loved my sister and right then all I wanted was for her to stop talking. I wasn't the same girl she knew. I was different and hurt physically and emotionally.

Chantal was the one person in my life I trusted and loved. As I looked at her, I started trembling. Crying and knowing how bad my situation was with high fever brought on by the infections from my many wounds, she said, "If you die, what will I do?"

Not wanting to cause undue worry, my father had decided not to tell Chantal and Valentine how serious my condition was and how uncertain was my prognosis. Neither knew, for example, that I had been in and out of a coma for more than 20 days or that the doctors had said there was only a small chance that I would live. Meanwhile, on his visits my father kept asking for my forgiveness. "Please, Christine, my daughter. I love you. I need you, and I don't want you to die," he said. "Please, little girl. I want you to know that I have changed. I am a good Christian. I believe in God, and I believe that my God will not let me down and will heal your body." As Chantal, at my insistence, had not told him or Valentine that I could talk and was not comatose, he didn't know that I heard every word he spoke. "I wish you would talk to me," he said. "I am sorry, and I hope someday I will have your forgiveness," saying that everything he had done to us as children was revenge for what our mother had done to him and to us before.

What signaled to me those times that I was coming out of my coma—not that I knew, of course, that I had been in a coma in real time—was the sense that I had been having dreams, especially nightmares. Being in a coma is like being in a dream, but without any dream memories. It was strange to think that almost an entire month of my life had vanished without a trace.

One day when I came out of my coma, my father was there to offer his support. He said how sorry he was that I was going through all this by myself and that he wished he could take my place so I could go home. After everything he had done and said to me all those years, now he was telling me that he wished he could take my place? I thought about what he was saying and started smiling. I looked at him as though maybe he really had changed, that maybe he honestly did feel remorse for how he had treated me.

Later that day Chantal came to see me. She was happy that I had come out of my coma and was getting better and said she knew I was going to be fine. I told her I wished I could share her optimism.

After spending several more weeks in King Faisal, I was finally able to go home, 14 years old by the calendar but, sadly, much older in all the ways that meant anything. The changes that awaited me at home were startling although not unexpected. My father was nice and respectful to all of us children, and Valentine was better with us, too, as when, for example, she would come into my room to talk (even though I didn't talk to her because I was still in "mute mode"), buy me nice clothes at the mall and help in my recovery from my wounds.

But as much as much as my physical and psychological wounds were healing, if slowly, I still had anger inside for what I and all the other innocents in my family had suffered. Why us? I asked. Why me? With all my anger and pain, it took a while to even try to be friendly with anyone, especial my father and Valentine. I felt miserable, that I didn't deserve to ever be happy, that there was no reason to live. Not only did I push people away, I had hate for them and didn't trust anyone. Even though I knew my father and Valentine had changed, I couldn't forget what they had done. Still, they were nicer to me, and I began to adapt to being around them. I was feeling bad about not talking to them and being angry after their efforts to apologize and help me recover, so it wasn't long before I began conversing with them in a normal manner.

11

RWANDA IN THE AFTERMATH

The three-month bloodletting that resulted in the killing of as many as one million Rwandans officially ended on July 17, 1994, the date RPF forces captured Kigali. At that time, the new government, led by President Kagame, and the international community began the long process of arresting, detaining and bringing to justice those responsible for the killings. In October 1994, the International Criminal Tribunal for Rwanda (ICTR), located in Tanzania, was established with the mandate to prosecute the crime of genocide, and in 1995 the tribunal began indicting and trying a number of high-ranking people for their role in the killings, although the process was made more difficult because the whereabouts of many suspects were unknown. Nevertheless, the trials continued over the next 15 years and included the 2008 conviction of three former senior Rwandan defense and military officials for organizing the genocide.

In addition, the gacaca courts have tried thousands of alleged *genocidaires* (and released thousands more) since being established in 2001, as they attempted, as one observer put it, to "eradicate the culture of impunity" in the country. Like many thousands of other Rwandan victims and relatives of victims, I opposed, and oppose, impunity for the criminals and killers who destroyed my country and my life and the lives of so many other innocent people. It was, and is, impossible for us to forget our friends and family lost, to pretend that nothing had happened to the blameless. No matter how hard we try, we cannot hold back the tears.

Today, hundreds if not thousands of fugitives indicted for war crimes in Rwanda are living freely in Africa and Europe while their victims and their victims' families continue to suffer and wait for justice.

Furthermore, ask yourself if you could live next to people who maimed, tortured and killed your fellow citizens, your friends and your family. Many "survivors" are survivors in name only, suffering from deep and lasting, even permanent, psychological and physical damage and other obstacles to their wellbeing. For me and many others in a Catholic and increasingly evangelical Rwanda, God has been my savior, literally. And while I now live in the U.S., I try to visit Rwanda every five years to pay my respects to my lost friends and family, but upon each visit the fear of being killed returns, as I know that I am a witness to those who killed my family 20 years ago and who may still be at large, ready to silence me for having lived through and seen their heinous and inhumane crimes. As one who no longer has to experience that fear on a daily basis, I feel sorry for Rwandans who are still targeted, harassed and taunted by the Hutu killers or their friends and thank God every day that I am free of that dread.

While the government tries, even today, to push for justice and reconciliation, mistrust and pain run deep in Rwandan society. Tutsi and Hutu alike say love and forgiveness are not possible, not even thinkable. I will never forget a visit I made in 1996 to a family, Emmanuel and Janet Kayitare, who had children my age I used to play with. As I came upon their house, the first thing I saw was that it had no roof, only a piece of plastic to protect those living there from the elements. In fact, I didn't even think anyone lived there, but when I knocked on the door, a woman came and hugged me and invited me in to sit down. Then her husband came out of another room. He was in a wheelchair and had lost both his legs in the massacre. When he saw me, he started crying and asked if I was OK. I was honest and told him no, I wasn't, but even though he and his wife had heard I was dead, he decided not to ask me any questions, which I was grateful for. I noticed that the house was quiet, that it didn't seem as though my friends were there, but I was afraid to say anything. Then Mr. Kayitare said: "I know why you are here, but all of our children are gone. They were killed. We are alone. We have lost everything, including our family." Then he said he wanted to die, that there was no purpose for him to be alive, except to fight for justice for his children. He told me that a nearby resident was the one who had killed his family and that he had just got out of jail and was back living in the neighborhood. Since his children's killer had returned, he said, he was sick and exhausted all the time and unable to deal with the emotional trauma caused by what the man had done and seeing him living free. I hugged the Kayitares and told them how sorry I was. I left their house and cried all the way home.

I felt lucky to be alive but also guilty at *being* alive, even though I had been through hell and had no logical reason to feel bad for having lived when so many had died. But there was no logic to anything at that time. Nothing made sense, and there were no means to reconcile the irreconcilable, within society or within ourselves. It seemed there wasn't a survivor who didn't wish he or she were dead. In a hundred days, millions of children were left without parents and grandparents, brothers and sisters. The injured and widows and widowers were struggling with depression and suicidal thoughts. The new government was trying to help, but the task before it was monumental and the resources miniscule. Besides, many survivors couldn't bear to relive the past. I don't blame them, because it has taken me 20 years to tell the story of my wretched life.

Writing this book has helped me become more open to others and feel better about myself, even though the pain at times is unrelenting, and no matter how hard I try or wish it were otherwise, the memories of what I lived through and what I lost refuse to go away. Now, thanks to many years of counseling, I have learned to embrace others, not push them away, to the point where I want to share my story and tell the world not only what happened to my country, but how I was able to survive, in every sense of the word.

12

JUSTICE QUESTIONED

Twenty years later, even though I am better, the truth is my life is still in pieces. How, when you have lived through what I have lived through, when you have seen what I have seen, when you have lost what I have lost, can it be otherwise? Another truth: I can neither forgive nor forget, not completely, and I will not live my life pretending that I can. To do so would be to dishonor everything and everyone that I have lost and everything my countrymen and women have lost. To do so would be to deny my reality and my history. This is something I do not choose to do.

It is not that I haven't tried. After years of therapy, praying and support, I was finally able to forgive my father for destroying my childhood. But that doesn't mean I will forget.

As a devout Christian, I know that Jesus said we should love our enemies, but I can't accept that. To be honest, I wish Rwanda had the death penalty because I want all those killers to be killed, just as they killed others. Hate is not too strong a word to describe my feelings toward them. In place of Jesus and his exhortation to love our enemies, I would put the Old Testament principle of an eye for an eye. Kill and be killed. That is how I feel.

Without the death penalty, the killers spend a few years in prison and then go back to live among their victims. And the victims will have received no justice, only bitterness and sadness. My friend Claudine was a child of 12 when the genocide started, and her two brothers were even younger. The three of them survived, but their parents, who were killed in front of them, did not, so Claudine and her brothers were orphaned, and Claudine had to care for herself and her brothers as a girl of 12. During the many years living in their parents' house by themselves, they had little or no support from the government and were forced to get by on next to nothing. When I saw her on a recent trip to Rwanda, Claudine told me that she still lives in fear and can never forgive or forget.

When I begin to feel sorry for myself, I think of Claudine and feel bad for her and try to help her as much as I can. I tell her I also will never forgive or forget, and she tells me that knowing she isn't alone in carrying around those feelings gives her consolation. How can one possibly recover from something like that? Today I am 34, a grown woman, but I still ask myself what happened in Rwandan society and in the world to cause a reign of terror and evil like that to occur and to rage unchecked for what seemed an eternity.

In 2001, the Rwandan government, struggling with the overwhelming task of trying tens of thousands of alleged *genocidaires,* established the gacaca to ease the government's burden. The aim of the system, a form of community justice, was and is to promote healing and reconciliation among all Rwandan citizens. Not everyone in Rwanda supports the gacaca courts. For many, it is hard to walk down the street knowing you may meet someone who killed your family, or to go to court to face the killer or killers.

Among Tutsis, many feel justice is not being served in the gacaca, and even some human rights organizations question the fairness of a system in which killers who confess are let off with no punishment because, in confessing, they are helping unclog an overloaded judicial system. And as is well known in Rwanda, some of the killers who have been convicted have returned to society vowing revenge on those who testified against them. They spent those years in jail and are angry with the people who put them there, so they come back looking to get even, and the victims, without any money, can't move to a different neighborhood, meaning the killers know exactly where to find them. Or you see them in the store or on the street. The very men who killed your family or chopped off your arms or legs (or toes)! Put yourself in such people's position. How would you feel about reconciliation or the "justice" you received?

Many survivors in Rwanda are afraid to speak their minds about the gacaca and other aspects of the country's judicial system. Maybe because I live in the U.S., or maybe because I'm a fighter at heart, I will not be silenced on the subject.

I remember how one of my friends, Agatha, a survivor, called me one day, telling me about a man who had killed her family. He was in jail for only seven years, and even before he was released, he started writing letters to Agatha and his other victims asking for forgiveness. After getting his release, the first thing he did was to go to his victims' homes to ask them for forgiveness in person. As Agatha told the story, it was a Sunday morning, and she was ready to go to church when there was a knock at her door. She was expecting a friend, but she was wrong. When she opened the door, she found herself face to face with the man who had killed her family. He was there to ask for forgiveness. She ran screaming and crying for help, saying her family's killer was on her doorstep. She was so frightened that she moved in with a friend and didn't return to her home for months.

Agatha told me how the killer said to her, "They were not all killed, after all." And Rwanda wants to talk about reconciliation? More than anything, Agatha said, was her yearning to leave Rwanda and start her life over "far away from here." I didn't blame her. I couldn't imagine coming face to face with the man who had slaughtered my brothers and sisters and parents. You are crying every day for your loss and then that mass murderer asks you to forgive him and not only that, threatens you in the same breath? That is not reconciliation! That is taking someone who is already terror stricken and forsaken and lost, and making her life even worse, if that were possible.

Having been through the hell of losing loved ones and seeing the horror of the genocide first hand, I can say it seems the Rwandan government doesn't care about how painful "reconciliation" is for the victims, that the people pushing it don't know what we went through and what they are asking us to go through again by not receiving justice and by having to live next to the killers of our families. To me, reconciliation is more than misbegotten; it is misguided, heartbreakingly, even criminally, so.

Here is another example of a victim who was victimized again. Valentine has a friend, Mutoni, who lost her husband and all six of her children in the genocide, and who, herself, suffered horrendous machete wounds that nearly killed her. Today, the Hutu women who are her neighbors and whose husbands committed the murders openly tell her they are sorry she survived, and their children do the same. Mutoni lives in fear of these women and their children and is frightened about what will happen to her when her family's killers return from prison. She is just one among thousands who see reconciliation as a failure, in practice and in principle. "I know most people think it is right to forgive," she said. "But how can you forgive people who killed your family and destroyed your life? We victims will never get justice for our loves ones, and we are forced to live with our killers. It isn't right."

Rwanda has problems in addition to the most serious one of the genocide, but if you see Rwanda today you will see that it has developed, and most people are moving on with their lives. On the surface everything looks normal. But the flowers that bloom have beneath them the dead, who will never be found or receive justice and whose memories will never be honored. As much as I love flowers, I never buy or even smell them there because of what they represent: a false, hollow rebirth. Today, every day, when I pray to God, I always put the victims and survivors in my prayers and ask God to help those who survived to somehow, someday be able to move on from their unspeakable pain in a way that honors everyone who suffered, living and dead together.

After all those months in the hospital recuperating from my many operations and infections, and following some time at my father's new house during which I realized I had to get away from the terrible memories of the genocide, I went to Europe to live with Leontina. Eventually, after spending time in Romania and France, I decided to go back to Africa to find Angelique, a promise and a gift I had made to myself. With financial help from Leontina, who knew how important this undertaking was for me, I flew back to Rwanda to begin my search. Nathalie had given me the name of the county in which she lived, and using that information, I was able to locate her house—only to discover that it had been burned to the ground. Thank God, Nathalie and Angelique had survived and escaped unharmed. I was conducting my search on foot, and it was frightening to be so susceptible to harm, as I knew how the Tutsi people were still at risk of attack by the Hutu. Nevertheless, now joined by Chantal and Valentine, I continued my quest, which led us to a different village, Byumba, in a different, distant county, where we asked people and knocked on doors until one day we met a nice woman who said, yes, she knew who Nathalie was and that she would take us to her house.

We walked a while, and before long, we were at Nathalie's house, whereupon I found myself seeing her again after all that time. Then Angelique walked into the room. Oh, God, how beautiful she was! Just the way I remembered her when I first saw her in that field next to her parents' bodies three years before. I asked her for a hug, and I couldn't help myself; I started crying just holding that beautiful child, knowing how loved she was in that house and how I had helped save her life. Chantal, Valentine and I accepted Nathalie's kind invitation to stay that night in her home, and I spent the whole time holding Angelique and telling her, and myself, how happy I was for her.

Thanks to Nathalie, I stayed in Angie's life for many years, sending her a card and a present on Christmas and on her birthday, a date Nathalie and I had improvised because we didn't know her real one.

A baby who almost died, Angie through her example helped me realize that there was such a thing as a second chance in life, and I became ever more thankful to have that chance and began thinking about who I wanted to be and what I wanted my future to look like, all because of that beautiful girl who opened my eyes to life's possibilities and the promise of new beginnings.

Our country was healing, even if it often seemed to be at the expense of the survivors. The government was working hard, if not always successfully, to keep the peace and make sure that people were safe. My family had changed, especially my father, who was now a practicing and devout Christian and a good family man. And I stopped using my stepmother's first name, calling her Mom just as Chantal had been doing.

13

MEETING MY BIOLOGICAL MOTHER FOR THE FIRST TIME

When I was in the hospital, I met a man, Steinar Johnson, who was with the UNHCR, the United Nations refugee agency, and we became friends. Steinar was someone I could share my problems with, and when I told him about my mother, he said he would help me find her. With financial assistance from him and information from my father, and my grandmother I went back to Romania, to Cluj-Napoca, to find the woman who had given birth to me but whom I had never known.

The address my father had given me for my mother turned out to be of no use, as she had sold the house and moved elsewhere. But I found Aunt Gina and Aunt Gabi and Uncle Mugur, and they put me up for a night and helped me locate my mother, who was living in another city. When we found her, Gina, who was my mother's older sister, told me to wait while she knocked on the door, saying my mother might have an unpredictable reaction to my sudden appearance. When my mother opened the door and was told I had come all the way from Africa to see her, she said that was impossible, that Chantal and I had died in the genocide, even though she had no way of knowing that as she had never made any effort to get in touch with Chantal or me or our father. My aunt called me over to the house, and there I was, just like that, standing before the woman I hadn't seen since being abandoned by her at birth, the mother who had never made a single attempt to check on me, the woman who had never acknowledged my existence or had told me she loved me.

I stood there trembling, not knowing what to do or to expect. Crying, my mother hugged and kissed me, and I remember thinking she loved me after all and that everything would be all right. Then, giving me a ring she was wearing, she said, "Now go back to where you came from!" I was so completely shocked by her words that I hardly knew what to do or say, so I said nothing and left with Gina. That night, while staying in my mother's city with some friends of Aunt Gabi, I thought about how my father used to tell Chantal and me that our mother never loved us but how I had thought he was making that up to make himself feel better. Now I saw that it was true. But then my mother surprised me: she called my aunt's friend's house and asked my aunt if I would consider spending some time with her. When Aunt Gabi asked me, I said no. But she said that maybe my mother had reacted the way she had out of shock and pleaded with me to give her a chance, which I then said I would do.

My mother came for me the next day, but the fact was that I had little interest in seeing her, or so I believed. Why set myself up for another psychological beating? I told myself. Looking at her, I had to admit that she was a beautiful woman. But still, I felt little or no connection to her. Nevertheless, when she asked me to stay in her house until I returned to Rwanda, I said yes, and we spent the next three weeks in close proximity—in close proximity, as well, to her five dogs and six cats, whom she called her "children"—trying to reconnect on a meaningful level. Unfortunately, my mother started telling lies about my father, which I knew were lies because he had shown me letters testifying to the truth of the matters in question. The biggest and most unforgivable lie was that she hadn't abandoned Chantal and me at all, that our father had "taken us" from her and that there was nothing she could do to stop it. I told her I knew that wasn't true and said all she was doing with her falsehoods was adding more pain to my life. "I suffered all my life missing you and wondering about you," I said, "but now I know that everything my father said about you was true." I was sobbing now, and said, "Chantal and I loved you and cried for you. Did you ever cry for us?"

That night I called Chantal and put her on the phone with our mother. Chantal told her she wanted to visit her and see the city where she was born, and my mother promised to prepare the paperwork to facilitate her trip.

Over the next several days, she continued to lie to me about her reasons for letting Chantal and me go back to Rwanda with our father. She claimed that as Romania was a poor country, she thought Chantal and I would have better opportunities in Rwanda (as if Rwanda were not a poor country) with my father and his extended family. She told me this without a trace of sorrow or regret, which astounded me. "You are the devil, and you have no heart," I screamed.

"I'm sorry to have upset you, Christine," she said. "But please understand and believe me when I say I love you and Chantal."

I said, "I am tired of all your lies, and when I leave here, I never want to see you again. You don't need Chantal and me; go and be happy with your dogs and cats." I told her how I had survived a massacre and she hadn't even asked me how or if I was OK emotionally, not even what my earlier life had been like. "I can say I got to see you, but otherwise I am sorry I came," I said. She listened to me and offered an apology, but it sounded empty, so I didn't even acknowledge it.

The next morning Mircea, my mother's boyfriend of many years, came over for coffee, assuming he and my mother were alone in the house. As she had never told him that she had children, she decided to hide me in another room. But when I suddenly appeared in front of them, Mircea said hello to me in Romanian, and when I didn't answer, my mother got worried about his finding out who I was. Then he asked her who I was. "She looks like you and talks like you," he said.

All my mother said was, "She's a family member," hoping to end the discussion, and adding that I would be leaving soon to go back home. He said maybe he could take us both out to dinner one night, but my mother said no. As Mircea was getting ready to leave, I blurted out, "Mom," and he said, "Oh, my Lord, this is your child? You never told me you had a daughter, and we've been together almost twenty years!" He was angry and asked me if Lillian was my mother. I said yes, and that I had a sister who was three years older than I. At this point, my mother started yelling at me and ordering me to my room. Now it was my turn to get angry. I looked at her and said, "No! I am not going to my room. Who are you to tell me what to do?" I told her if she wanted, I would move into a hotel, change my airplane ticket and go back early. Then Mircea started asking me questions about where I'd grown up, and when I told him he became visibly emotional, but when he saw I didn't want to talk about it, he said he understood and didn't ask any more questions. He asked me if my father were still around, and I told him yes and that he had taken another wife. Mircea showed more emotion and concern about me than my mother did. She was crying, but I knew it was only because she had got caught in her lies, not because she was sad for me.

My mother and Mircea had a business together that had been named for me. Mircea said to my mother, "Remember when we opened that business and we were trying to find a name for it, and you kept saying Christine & Nova? I knew on that day you were hiding something from me because it was odd that you wanted that name for the business, not our names together." He said, "Lillian, you should be happy that your girls are alive and safe and that one of them is here with you and wants a relationship with you after everything you have done." My mother didn't say anything. From the things he said and did, Mircea, I could tell, was a good man,

My mother told me that she still loved my father and that that was why they had never got divorced. At one point after they separated, she said, she started telling him that she wanted him and Chantal and me back and that he must leave Valentine and their children, but by then it was too late.

After those several contentious weeks with my mother, I left Romania and went back to Rwanda. When it was time for Chantal to visit her, she went to the Romanian embassy in Kenya to ask for a visa, but they said our mother had sent them a letter saying she didn't want Chantal to come. We couldn't believe she would do such a thing, this being a woman who had, after all, promised her daughter she would apply for a visa for her. But it was true: she was turning her back on her daughter once again. It was so very sad.

A few years later, I paid a second surprise visit to my mother, but this time I let my visa expire while I was there, so I couldn't go back, a plan my father had cooked up to punish my mother for doing what she had done to Chantal. I wanted to become a Romanian citizen so that I could help Chantal visit in the future. When my visa expired, my mother became worried and was right to become so: when we went to the immigration office, they said they could not renew my visa and that my mother should begin the process of obtaining my Romanian citizenship. Later, as soon as I received my papers, all I could think was, yes! I won!

Around that time, Chantal met a man her age and got pregnant. When my father found out, he threw her out of the house, but then, when she became ill, he invited her back, but she ended up losing the baby. She left her boyfriend and started college, where she met a student with whom she became friends. But this "friend" was disrespectful to Chantal, although she didn't mind it that much because she had come to think it was normal for a man to beat a woman. When I kept reminding her that that was not acceptable and certainly not normal, she started becoming distant and began to hide things in her personal life from me.

14

GRIEVING AND THE LOSS
OF MY SISTER

In 1999, when I was almost 19 and living in Constanta, Romania, I met a man who worked for the American Refugee Committee, an NGO that had been set up after the genocide to help with the Rwandan refugee crisis. The man, David Williams, a 40-year-old American from St. Louis, Missouri, was a country director for ARC and a kind, caring man. We started dating and, before long, fell in love. Soon, though, David was reassigned to Guinea-Conakry, a country in West Africa. He asked me to go with him. Not feeling ready to uproot myself, I said no and had to bear the pain of not having this wonderful man in my life. After he had been in Guinea for a while, he again asked me to join him, and this time I said yes. It wasn't long before we got married and began talking about having a family. But I couldn't get pregnant, with this unfortunate situation continuing for years. Nevertheless, David would always tell me that we would have a child some day. Chantal had started dating a young Belgian I had known in Kigali by the name of Michel. I had never liked Michel. During the time he and Chantal were dating, he was cheating on her, but she refused to break up with him. Then one day they were out driving and Michel leaned over, flung open Chantal's door and pushed her from the car into the middle of the street; she ended up in the hospital where doctors needed stitches to close an injury to her head.

After this incident, I begged Chantal to come and live with David and me in Guinea. But she didn't feel she wanted to leave Rwanda and her friends, especially since Michel had apologized and pleaded with her to resume their relationship, which, over my and my family's strong objections, she, thinking that Michel would never mistreat her again, agreed to do. Tragically, events would prove her wrong.

In June 2002, Michel and Chantal were in Uganda, where Michel was set to take part in an amateur car race, when they had a big fight in front of their friends, and Chantal broke off their relationship right then and there. Michel told her if he couldn't see her, no one could. Later that day, as Chantal rode in Michel's car on the way back to Kigali, there was an accident, and both driver and occupant were killed instantly. Chantal, my loving sister, was only 25.

A week before the accident I talked to Chantal, and she told me she thought something bad was going to happen to her, as though she knew she were going to die. She said, "Christine, I want you to know that I love you, and I will always love you. Please pray for me." When I asked her why she was saying those things, she said that she and Michel had been fighting all the time because she thought he had started cheating again. I told her she was a beautiful women and to just pack her things and go. I also told her that we had been through so much together and that I would always be there for her. I said, "If you need *anything*, just let me know." Those were the last words I spoke to her.

Later that day I received an email from Chantal telling me what was really going on, namely, that because Michel was treating her badly, she was going to leave and go back to our father's house. All that week I had unbearable back pain along with weird dreams about Chantal. In the dreams she was wearing a long white dress. Looking back on my dreams and my pain later, I realized I was having premonitions. On the day Chantal died, I decided to call her to repeat my invitation to her to stay with David and me. When she didn't answer her phone, I called Valentine and then my father. Neither one of them answered their phones either. I tried to reach Chantal all that day until finally someone, a stranger, answered and said she didn't know anyone by the name of Chantal. I said but this is her phone number. The woman hung up on me. I called her back and asked her to tell me what was going on. Please, I said, becoming more and more worried. Just tell me if my sister is OK; I don't care about the phone. She hung up again.

Now my worry had turned to fear. I knew—I could *feel*—that something was wrong. My hands shaking, I called Michel but an unknown voice also answered his phone. When I asked for Michel, he said he didn't know a Michel and that I had dialed a wrong number. By then I was in tears, begging this man to tell me how it was that he had Michel's phone. He said all he knew was that there had been an accident and that someone had sold the phone to him. I asked where the accident was, and he said on a highway in Mbarara, which was a town in western Uganda. I started screaming and yelling and saying to this voice to please tell me everyone was all right. He said, "The white guy died there, but the girl was still moving when the ambulance picked her up."

By that time I was hysterical. I called David, and he came home from work and started making phone calls. I said, "I knew something was going on, or else why did I have all those dreams?" I said, God, please protect my sister. How could she die after surviving the genocide? I said to him. You will not let her die, just like that. I kept asking David what will happen to me if Chantal were gone. Please, David, tell me, I said and kept grabbing his shirt and clutching his face. He looked at me and said he loved me and I said, please, I want my sister, at least to talk to her and hear her voice.

I was beside myself with dread and so was David, who was crying with me. I said maybe Chantal wasn't with Michel because she'd told me a few days before that he was cheating again and that she was leaving him. Pray that the woman in car was somebody else, not my Chantal, I said.

I got the shattering news of Chantal's death from my mother. My father had called her in Romania to tell her and then asked her to call me, as he had been unable to reach me. My mother called and sounded weird and asked me if I was all right. I said no, and then, without saying anything more, she asked to speak to David, which was strange because I knew she hated him. I passed the phone to David, and as I stood there I saw him listening and then saw his face turn completely white. He hung up the phone and looked at me and told me to sit down. I said I was not sitting down, just tell me what's wrong and tell me now. David came over to me and he said, "Honey, your sister is gone." All I could think to say was, "Gone where?" He told me she had passed away. He put his arms around me and held me. I am so sorry, he said. I was screaming and literally kicking the walls. I was as close to being in shock as was possible without actually going into shock. Chantal was my life, and now she was dead. I thought of all that she and I had gone through and everything we had lost and for her to die like that was pain beyond all imagining. If not for having David in my life, I know this was something I would not have survived.

By the time I got back to Rwanda, the funeral had taken place. I didn't get a chance to say goodbye to my best and closest friend. Later, when I went to the graveyard with flowers, I started screaming when I saw Chantal's name and the fresh concrete with its cross and passed out. My friends took me home, but I simply didn't care anymore. I had given up and hadn't eaten since Chantal died and was hospitalized for a week for a malnutrition-related illness. There I was, again, in a hospital, my father sitting next to me and me crying to him that he was not my father, he was a monster, I don't want to see you, I hate you. It was as if I were 15 again and recovering from my injuries from the genocide. I will never forget what you did to Chantal and me, I said. My father said that he thought I had forgiven him a long time ago. Please, he said, I am a good Christian, a better man. I am so sorry. Chantal was my daughter, and I lost her. Please don't push me away. I need you, he said. I love you.

It may seem cold hearted in light of what he was saying, but my feelings for my father at that moment were probably at their lowest ever, and they were always very, very low. "Leave me alone," I said.

"My friends are dead and now Chantal." I told him I didn't need a father—especially him—to help me. Just the opposite, as he made me remember how terrible, because of him, Chantal's and my childhood had been, so not only was he not helping me by being in my life, he was making things worse.

When I got out of the hospital, I was in bad shape. I was living on pure feeling, and that feeling was depression. For six months, I talked to myself all the time and gave David reason to have grave concerns about me, especially about leaving me alone during his many work-related trips abroad. That was when he came up with the idea of having someone from my family stay with me, and I said that maybe I should give my mother another chance and see if, were she to come to Africa, she could help me, and we could have a loving relationship. We called her, and she said she would come, but as I found out later, it was more because she was excited to be in Africa than it was to see me. Even so, when she arrived in Conakry, where David and I waited for her, the first few days she was good to me. But she wanted to go out, and soon she started hanging out with my girlfriends and would be gone all day, leaving me alone, and when she got home, she would come and sit by my bed to talk to me for ten minutes and tell me Christine, we are all going to die someday, including you, so stop crying about your sister. She is gone and will never come back. Then she would get up, and I would be all alone again. I felt she was as heartless as it was possible to be, but then, where my mother and her children were concerned, "heart" had nothing to do with it.

One day my friend Ornella showed up and invited me to go out to a restaurant, but I told her I couldn't, that I had lost a lot of weight and could barely stand up, which she already knew. She said, OK, I will take Lillian out somewhere. I reminded Ornella why David and I had asked my mother to come in the first place—to be with me. Then Ornella turned on me and said I was jealous of my mother because she was having fun and that she couldn't believe a daughter would be jealous of her own mother. I thought, first my mother, then my friends.

That night, it got even worse. My mother announced she was

going to go drinking and dancing with a group of people. Hearing this, I became angry and upset and told her I didn't want her in my house and that I was tired of her always putting me down and criticizing me about losing Chantal. I said who are you to criticize me when you never knew her, you never saw her, and you abandoned her when she needed you most. "I gave you a chance," I said. "I paid your ticket to come and stay with me while David was away. But now I am done. Pack up and go." Then I told her I remembered when Chantal wanted a visa to come to Romania to see her, and what did she do? "You went behind her back and wrote to the embassy in Nairobi telling them not to give her a visa, and you lied to her. And now you are standing here in my house telling me that I am complaining?"

Then I said to Ornella, who had been my friend for many years, that I was there for you when your husband was bad to you, I was there for your children, and I loved you, but from today you are no longer welcome in my house and don't ever call me because I am done with you. She tried to apologize, but I told her to leave. While she was leaving I called to her and said, "Aren't you forgetting something?" She gave me a puzzled look. "My mother," I said. "Take her with you, and please don't come back, either of you. Let me live in my misery without you."

My mother packed up and departed with Ornella, and I was embarrassed to tell David that they had left together or that all the time he was traveling my mother was in bars and night clubs running around like a teenager and that she didn't care about me or spend any time with me, instead asking if she could wear my clothes, which I answered by saying I only shared my clothes with my sister, no one else, and most certainly not her.

I had been wrong about giving her a second chance. She was a selfish, mean and unhappy woman, and every time I gave her an opportunity to be a real mother, she disappointed me, so I gave up on her, deciding to let her live her life in *her* misery. And yet, despite everything, I still love her even today, which is something I can't understand or actually believe.

When David came home a few days later and asked where "Mom" was, I told him she had left at my insistence. "The whole time you were gone, she was hanging out in bars or telling me how stupid I was to be sad about Chantal, so I told her to leave," I said. After I told David this, he said he had had a bad feeling all along and that I shouldn't feel it was something I had to hide from him. "That woman was never there for you, Christine," he said. "What made you think she would be there for you now?" At that point I didn't know what to say, so I stayed very quiet but very sad.

At David's suggestion, we called Ornella to see if my mother was still staying with her. After telling us that she was, Ornella apologized to me for her mean words and for her interactions with my mother, saying all she had been trying to do was get me out of the house to help bring some positivity into my life. She then said she wanted my mother out of *her* house, so over David's mild opposition, I agreed to let her come back to stay with the two of us until she returned to Romania, which would be in just a few days. During those days, my time with her was marked by tolerance at best, and ill feelings simmering just out of sight at worst. I do giver her credit for not criticizing me, which was a major improvement over her usual conduct.

With my mother back home, a safe 5,000 miles away, I turned all my thoughts to Chantal. It was as if part of me had died with her, and her presence in the house, an angel watching over and protecting me, was something I felt deeply. I continually prayed that she would have peace. It took many years of grieving for her before my emotional world regained a semblance of normalcy even as I knew that life without her would never be the same because she had been all I had, other than David. I was angry and sad all the time, in tears almost every day, losing weight and talking to myself about why had she abandoned me and given up her promises to me. I realized on some level that I was being selfish, but I also knew that my deepest sorrow was for Chantal and the life she would miss out on.

I would talk to her and call out her name every day and say if she heard me to know that I loved her. A part of me even felt she was going to come back, surprise me and show up on my doorstep. Another part of me knew this was completely irrational, but, then, nothing about my life, except for David, seemed to be rational in any way, so my thoughts seemed somehow normal. It was a long time before I came to accept the reality that Chantal was gone forever and that all I could do was pray for her soul and start to try to put my life together, yet again.

I knew I needed help, and I thank God for David, who worried about me, was there for me, cared for me, loved me. He would make food—noodle soup, beef casseroles—that he knew I loved and beg me to eat, something I tried to do to make him happy. He would constantly tell me how much he loved me and that he would be with me forever. I felt even though he was my husband he was also my best friend, and knowing that helped save me, of that I am sure. Together with Chantal, he was the only person I could trust and depend on as I tried to come to terms with the past.

Whenever I felt like giving up, David would urge me not to lose hope, telling me to focus on the present and saying how much he believed in me. With his help and support, I began to regain my health, to feel more confident about myself and to realize that I could accomplish things, that all that was holding me back was the negativity that had been my life as a child and young adult.

I knew someone who had lost his entire family in a car accident. He told me that at first he was so anguished he pushed everyone away who was trying to help him and who loved him. But then he realized that keeping everything inside was the worst thing he could do, so he sought out counseling and renewed old friendships and slowly began to come out of his depression. I decided to try that in my own life and was glad I did.

One time when I was in Kigali and visiting my family at my father's house, I noticed how no one talked about Chantal, as though she had never existed. Then, as I looked around the house, I saw pictures of my stepbrother and grandmother who had died in the genocide but not a single picture of Chantal. I felt a voice screaming inside of me. Maybe I was envious of them for the way they could move on. Or maybe I hated them for the way they could move on. I only know that I wanted to get out of that house and find someplace to hide, to run away from my pain and the people causing it. For all the sorrow and sickness I felt during and after the genocide, those feeling s were nothing compared to the emptiness I felt after Chantal died, when my life, except for David, became a void.

More than 10 years later, I still grieve for her and even though I have already cried a sea of tears, I know my longing for her will not end until I am with her again.

I miss so many things about her, mostly the times we spent talking. There was nothing we could or would not share because we knew, having lived through what we lived through, that life was too precious and fragile to take for granted. We would talk on the phone for hours until David would good-naturedly complain that he was hungry or it was late and he was tired. He would often fall asleep to the sound of my voice in the loving embrace of my adored Chantal.

15

DOING GOOD AND HELPING OTHERS ARE THE KEYS TO HAPPINESS

At long last, I became pregnant, one of the few times in my life I was truly happy. David and I had been trying for so many years to have a baby that we had all but given up on the idea, and I said that even if we didn't have children, there were so many we could help who had been orphaned in the genocide or who had been abused and were in foster homes, that I would be happy with that. All I wanted was a child to love and protect.

Other countries also had problems with orphans. I remember vividly when I saw a little girl outside a mall in Bucharest. It was winter, and she didn't have shoes or a coat. I put my arms around her and asked her her name and then took her into the mall. The rich people there laughed at this dirty girl dressed in rags, but I didn't care. I took her to a store and bought her a new pair of shoes and a jacket and then took her to a restaurant and bought her lunch, which was when I finally saw her smile. Sadly, she reminded me of myself as a child, wearing dirty clothes, my body covered with bruises, with no one to care for me. Afterward, I put her in my car and told her to show me where she lived. When we arrived at her "house," it turned out to be a foster-care facility filled with other abandoned or orphaned children.

I spoke with someone there and told her how wrong it was to neglect these children, to not provide for them, to not have them attending school. I thought of how David and I had tried to adopt a Romanian child but were told we couldn't because David was an American. And here were these poor children deprived of a loving home all because of some politician's narrow mind.

This was around the time David and I were losing all hope of having a baby. He had been sent to Iraq—the year was 2003—and would come home every six weeks. It was during those visits that I became pregnant, although I didn't find out till later, and with the war becoming more and more frightening, I would become extremely worried for David's safety. I'd lost Chantal, and now my husband was in a war zone.

Later, David was posted to the Green Zone in Baghdad and couldn't call me as much as before, so I tried calling him but without success, and no one would tell me anything. I called his father in Oklahoma; he was worried about him, too. Just as when Chantal died and I couldn't reach her, I was scared that maybe David was dead and that that was why my calls weren't being answered. Then one day he called and said he was OK but that he couldn't talk. The relief I felt can't be put into words. "Promise me you will come home safe," I said. David said he would. "I love you, and you are my life," he told me. Then he said, "Christine, if I don't make it out of here alive, remember, you gave me a marriage and love I never could have imagined existed. But I promise, I will come home alive." He said he kept a picture of me in his pocket and kissed it 10 times a day.

I worried about David all the time and wanted him home safe with me. Meanwhile, even though my friends were kidding me about my round stomach, I told them I had given up on getting pregnant after so many years. But as I noticed my clothes getting smaller, I went to the doctor and found out that I was, indeed, three months pregnant. I couldn't believe it! Deliriously happy, I raced home and called David. Playing coy, I asked him when he was coming home, and he said in a few weeks, wondering if everything was OK. When I teased him about why he was asking, he said, "Because you seem so happy. Your voice is different. What's making you so happy, Christine?"

"I have a big surprise for you," I said. When he asked what it was, I said, "What do you think would make me happy?"

"Me!" he said, with a laugh.

I said, "Yes, honey, you make me happy. But I'm talking about something else."

He said, "Christine, after everything you've been through, if you could have a baby, that would make you happy."

"Yes, David," I said, "that would make me happy."

"Honey, are you pregnant? Please tell me."

When I told him, he was overwhelmed—for the baby, for himself, but mostly for me. "I can't wait to come home, Christine. We are finally having a baby!"

As happy as David and I were, I had a difficult pregnancy and spent much of the time in the hospital. Nevertheless, on Nov. 27, 2004, with David helping, I gave birth to a healthy baby boy David and I named Shawn, a name we chose for no other reason than that we liked it. It was the start of my new life as a mother and a happy, fulfilled woman. Words like "hope" and "new beginning" were now part of my life for the first time in memory.

I told myself this was why I survived the massacre. To have a baby and to bring happiness into the lives of people I loved.

David, the baby and I moved to Amman, Jordan, for a while so that David could see Shawn more often, but later Shawn and I moved to Romania. After we left Amman, suicide bombers attacked the hotel we had been staying in and where David was still staying. Thank God, he was all right.

During this time, David was traveling all over the world for ARC, and Shawn and I would go with him whenever we could. We were a very happy family.

My purpose, I felt, was to give Shawn a happy life, the life I never had, so I doted on him and became a supermom, always giving him the best birthday and Christmas celebrations possible—celebrations I never had—and, with David, doing everything within my power to give him a positive, loving upbringing.

As a husband and a father, David was more than I could have ever wanted. He was my lover and my best friend, he cooked for us when he was home, he helped with Shawn, and he was always available to listen to me and hold me when I was in need. He trusted me, and I trusted him. He treated me like a princess. I always felt safe with him and believed I was the luckiest woman in the world to have a husband like him. Shawn was happy and healthy, and we had lots of friends. In those wonderful times, when I looked back on my earlier life, I was at once in disbelief and eternally grateful that I was living amid such happiness. God, you have brought your light into the darkest of places, I said.

When Chantal and I were teens, I made the most unlikely of promises: I said if I ever went back to Romania, I would build a house for us to live in. And that is just what I ended up doing. Because David had worked hard his entire life, we had saved money, and he and I were able to build a nice house in Constanta, then as now the third-largest city in Romania and a popular resort on the Black Sea. I knew that my mother would not like us to be in Constanta, just five minutes from where she lived, but that was one of the very reasons I built the house there in the first place! I never even told her we were living there, and she didn't find out for years. Building that house was something I wanted to do for Chantal, to fulfill my promise to my best friend, who never got to go back to her birth country or see the mother she hardly knew.

When finished, our house was the most beautiful on the street, a home that I knew Chantal would have loved to live in. Eventually, my mother found out we were living so close to her, and during a rare visit, she became angry at us for being so secretive, but David defended me, saying he'd wanted to live there, too, and it was our money, so we could do what we wanted. His answer made her even angrier, but without anything to disparage about our happy family life, she resorted to criticizing David for the age difference between us, saying he should be ashamed of himself and why didn't he choose a woman his own age to marry. David looked at her and said, "Lily, do you think you should criticize us when you abandoned your children? Do you think Chantal died happy? Your own daughter who never got to know you? After you wrote to the embassy that you didn't want her here?" He spoke to her not in anger but in sadness. "Look in the mirror and think about yourself before you criticize anyone else." I was so proud of him for what he said and for how he stood up for me and Chantal. My mother couldn't think of anything to say; after all, there was no way she could defend how she had treated us. Instead, she pouted. "I am done. I am leaving and don't ever call me."

I told her if that was what she wanted, then that was what she would get. I said I was happy now and that she should want to be part of our family and get to know her only grandchild, but that if she wanted to go, I wasn't going to stop her. As she left, I called to her that she had forgot to apologize to David. She said she didn't have anything to apologize for. I said, fine, if you don't want to apologize then you will never be a part of my life or my son's life, ever. I told her that I had given her many chances to make amends, and that she had refused to change or apologize for her treatment of us, so, I said, go and be miserable. I am choosing to be happy.

After that, I didn't see her for several years, until one day I went grocery shopping near our respective homes, and we saw each other in the store. She came over to say hello, and we exchanged small talk for a while. She then asked if she could visit David, Shawn and me at our home some day, to which I said she could but only if she were to apologize to David for her criticism of him years before, which she said she would do. I was wary of giving her yet another chance after all the previous ones had ended up hurting me or my family, but when she came to the house, she did what she had promised: she told David she was sorry, asked for his forgiveness and said it would never happen again. His usual gracious self, David accepted her apology, saying the incident was in the past and what was important was that she said it would never happen again.

My wariness seemingly misplaced (for the first time in memory where she was concerned), I told my mother she was welcome to visit whenever she wanted. The more time that she spent with us, the better her relationship was with Shawn, who came to like her a lot. My relationship with her improved, too, and I was happy to have her around, especially when David was in Iraq, as he was a lot at that time. Often during her visits, she would cook traditional Romanian and French food for us, helping forge a stronger bond with Shawn and me, and with David when he was home.

Then one day she announced that she had broken up with Mircea and was dating a guy "younger than you, Christine." I couldn't believe my mother would do something as ridiculous as that. She was 53 and her new boyfriend, Frolin, was only 22, four years younger than I and an unbelievable 31 years younger than my mother! Still, when they came to my house to play with Shawn and cook, everything was fine, at least for a while. Soon, though, whether it was because of dating Frolin or something else, Lillian completely lost interest in us and pushed David, Shawn and me away. For years after, she never returned any of my calls. It was especially sad because Shawn had been getting closer and closer to her. It was also very hard for me to let her go, but I couldn't force her to choose us. Her decision was one I think she came to regret. But I guess she preferred dating that man to having a relationship with her family.

The past is for me the heaviest of burdens. To relive it is to invite the worst sorrow imaginable into my life. To ignore it is to let it infect my heart and mind. Especially when I was younger, I was too frightened to let my memories come back. All I wanted was to forget and move on. But as I get older, I am learning how hard that is to do, whether it's saying a prayer every April for family and friends who lost their lives in my country or my visits there every five years when I can't help reliving what I lived through: brutality and annihilation on a terrifying scale, the seemingly unlimited capacity of humans to do evil.

For many years, I had the same dream. There is a couple with two small children who are walking by the side of a road in Remera not far from where I am hiding. Some Interahamwe waiting in ambush grab them and then, ignoring the parents' cries for mercy, push them to the ground and cut their heads off in front of their children, who run away screaming. From my hiding place, I pray that the children survive. I tried everything to stop dreaming that dream—therapy, asking God, trusting in others, everything. Even though I eventually stopped having that dream, nothing I have done to keep my real-life traumas in the past has worked. Today, I have no desire to associate with people who survived the genocide because all they want is to talk about the past, while all I want is to live my life in the here and now. In fact, I don't have any friends who are survivors; all my close friends died or were never found. All I want for those of us who survived is to have happiness in our lives. And while I can't speak for others, I will not give up. I will keep searching for happiness, and with help from God I will find it.

Even though I cannot completely ignore the past and do "revisit" it every April and during my trips to Rwanda, I have never liked being questioned about the genocide, and knowing this, David never asked me about it, instead waiting many years for me to be able to tell him. He was patient and knew that when I was ready to talk about that dark chapter of my life, he was the first person I would reach out to.

Forgetting is the hardest thing. I remember one time when I went back to Rwanda and everyone was desperate to find their loved ones to give a proper burial to. It was 1996, and I was 17. I was walking in the devastated Kimironko district in Kigali and seeing people searching through piles of bodies, many of them dismembered, on the streets, to find their lost family and friends to take them home to say goodbye.

As I walked, I couldn't believe that more than two years after the genocide, bodies by the thousands had yet to be removed by the authorities from where they had fallen, and it seemed as if I were experiencing the genocide all over again. I started feeling weird and cold and couldn't see. The world was spinning. I thought someone was going to kill me. There it was again: my memory and my past hunting me down. I sat on the side of the road, my hands wrapped around my legs and my head bowed down. Remembering and reliving when all I wanted was to forget. I realized the past would always be with me, always be a part of my life. I told myself I would have to learn to live with it. While I was sitting there, a group of women walked by and saw me. They were nice and asked if I was all right, but I looked at them and said please leave me alone. They refused to go and kept asking me if I was sick or if I needed anything. Then one of them told me where they were going, saying do you see on the other side of the street where those people are digging? All my children and my family are there, she said, so we are digging them out. I looked, and there were hundreds of bodies piled up, like wood. "I am all alone," the woman said. "Everyone in my life is gone."

I said that is why I am sitting here. "Someone told me my friends Giselle and Josiane are in there," I said. I said all my past comes back to me, and I feel as if I am reliving 1994. The woman hugged me and calmed me down, and I felt comfortable talking to her. Then, as I listened to her story, I thought she had had it worse in the genocide even than I did.

I never should have taken that walk because of the terrible memories it brought back. I told a doctor once that I would give everything to be able to forget my past because in my entire life I had nothing good to remember. The doctor said, "You can live with your past by sharing your experiences with those you love." He also said that whenever I am despondent, I should write down exactly how I feel, that that would help me let go of the past. Maybe that is one reason I have written this book.

During the massacre I promised God that if I survived I would become a practicing Christian and help others who had experienced traumas of their own. I believe that God saved me and gave me a child and a husband and a good life for a reason and that he has a purpose for me. In Romania at that time there were many orphans who needed love and assistance from others. I started helping these children, inviting them to stay with David, Shawn and me for the holidays and have a warm bed and presents and love. Before that, I used to send money to the orphanages, but when I found out it was being used for things not related to the children, I changed my approach. I loved having those children in my home. I would look at them and say to myself I know how it feels to be without a family. Even with all the pain in my life, I knew I had to be strong for those children, and I also realized that that was a form of therapy and healing for me, as I loved the children deeply.

David would cook for them and feed them and read stories to them. They would sit in a circle and play games together and love spending time with us in our home. But soon they would have to go back to the same life they had before, and on that day I would cry and feel bad and wish I had done something more to help them. I asked David if we could adopt some of the children, including a baby that had been abandoned by her parents, and we started thinking about the ones we wanted until we found out we couldn't adopt because of David's nationality. We were heartbroken for ourselves, but even more for the children. Even so, we continued doing what we could to help them. Knowing these children had been on the streets, abandoned, maybe beaten and abused, reminded me of my own childhood, so I wanted to love and protect them in ways I had dreamed of but never known.

16

THE LOSS OF MY HUSBAND

It was 2008 when David came to Romania from Bagdad after our house in Constanta was built. He had the entire summer off, which gave us a lot of uninterrupted time together, something rare in our lives, so he invited his whole family, including his sister and her sons from Bangladesh and his father and brother from the States, to visit us, to enjoy the beach and the resort life. David was great with Shawn, who was three and a half, and we had a wonderful summer with his family. At the same time, David was preoccupied and worried. He would say things like "Everything will be fine" and "Christine, I trust you. I know you are a very good mother, that you will make good decisions." I would ask him what he was talking about, was something wrong, did he have an illness, what was going on?

He wouldn't tell me much, but he did say he felt "weird," that he was in a "different world "and that he thought something bad was going to happen. I thought maybe it had something to do with his being in Iraq, since he had been there from the very beginning of the war, or that maybe he was fearful of being hurt, or worse, when he went back. With his family in Constanta, including his father Wald, who was 93 and had cancer, and despite his preoccupations, David busied himself making sure everyone was having a good time. But afterward, he would share his concerns with me again, and, often, start crying. One day he asked me if I would make his favorite beef soup for him and the family, adding that, "From today, I want to eat all my favorite foods and do all the things I love, because who knows what the future holds."

I looked at him and said, "David, I am not happy hearing you talking like that. I feel as if I don't know you anymore. You're scaring me." I asked him if he was saying he wanted to divorce me or if he were planning to go somewhere without me.

He said, "Christine, you are the love of my life. I will never leave you or divorce you. I love you and Shawn now, and I will love you after I am gone."

I said, gone? Gone where? He said, "Gone as in dead" and then asked where I got the idea that he was leaving, repeating his vow of love for me and Shawn. Then he said he was worried that something bad might happen to him in Iraq, that so many people were getting injured and killed there, that his words had nothing to do with me. He asked me if I was happy in our marriage, and I told him yes but that my past was always in the back of my mind and that sometimes I'd get sad and cry, but I was stronger now because of him and Shawn. Then David hugged me and he said he would always love me in no matter what and said, please, Christine, remember everything I am telling you just in case I will never have a chance to talk to you again. I was trembling with worry and fear for him and our family.

Even though he was sad and anxious, David, with his father and others there, tried to make everyone happy, despite sleepless nights and little desire to eat even his favorite meals or enjoy himself. For me, hearing David saying repeatedly that he thought he wouldn't come back from Iraq was becoming increasingly hard to bear. One morning when I felt more drained than usual by his frightening words, I said, "You know what? I lost my sister in a car accident and my friends and relatives in the genocide, my parents never loved me, my father abused and beat me, and I survived a massacre. You and Shawn are my first real chance at happiness, so, David, please don't say those things."

He apologized, but he didn't stop, because he couldn't. He said he had "no idea" why he was having his premonitions, that he hated upsetting me and that "maybe" he would feel better soon. One day, when he was cooking one of his favorite meals, couscous, for everyone, he asked me to watch how he was making it. "When Shawn grows up," he said, "I want you to pass along the recipe to him so he can cook it for his wife." I said, "No, David, you will give him the recipe yourself."

He told me how, if something happened to him, he wanted me to move to the U.S. to be closer to his relatives. "I want Shawn to grow up knowing his American family," he said. Then he said what was the most distressing thing of all: "Please, Christine, I want you to find happiness. I want you to find another man."

I was so upset I hardly knew what to say, so I spoke the truth: "I will do everything you want, but I will never get married again, and I will never want anyone else in my life. I love you, and I want you to be there for me. Your son needs you. We all need you. I'm sorry." He told me again I should move on without him, that there was nothing wrong with finding happiness.

At the end of the summer his family left, so David, Shawn and I were alone again in our house. All I wanted was to help David feel good about himself before going back to Baghdad. I told him that he was not going to die and was going to be around for a very long time. But no matter what I said I couldn't get him to change how he felt. On the day before he left, I saw him with Shawn, holding him in his arms and talking to him, telling him how much he loved him and asking him to take care of me. The next morning, as we were getting ready to leave for the airport, he said, "I feel as if I'll never see this house again."

"David, what made you say that?" I said. All he could say was that he didn't know, but, then, a few minutes later, he became very quiet and started crying and looking sad. Soon after that, while on the highway, he abruptly announced that he wanted to go back to see the house one more time. I told him if we did that he might miss his flight and then get fired for returning to Baghdad late, and he said he didn't care, that he wanted to see the house again. When we arrived, we got out, and David, putting his arm around me, said, "Christine, we did a great job together; we have a beautiful home and a perfect family." I said yes, that's true, and that Shawn and I would be waiting for his return.

Then he turned to me and said he had changed his mind and wasn't leaving that day, repeating his stated indifference about possibly losing his job. As a result, we got to spend an extra week together, which was wonderful.

Then, with David once again in Iraq, my back pain and loss of appetite returned, and I began to feel lonely, just as before. The first thing I did every morning was turn on CNN to see if there had been any attacks in Baghdad. I would worry all day, every day. That was my life while David was living in a war zone.

I kept my phone in my pocket all the time and would try to call him but he wouldn't or, more often, couldn't answer. That didn't stop me: I would call headquarters and talk to some of his friends just to make sure he was safe. Amid my worry and fear, thank God I had Shawn, who always made me happy, and we used our time together to build a stronger bond than ever between us. One time around then, David returned to the States to visit his family. When he and I talked on the phone, I could tell he wasn't well, and Mark said I should come right away, with neither he nor David telling me what was wrong. Without even packing, I grabbed Shawn and the necessary papers, raced to the airport and boarded a flight to St. Louis.

When I talked to David briefly before leaving for the U.S., he'd struggled with remembering things and repeatedly said his name rather than answer my questions, which greatly upset me. Then, when Shawn and I arrived in St. Louis, Mark wouldn't tell me anything, not even that David was in the hospital, so I had to spend a long, lonely, terrifying night not knowing what was wrong with my husband. The next morning Mark took Shawn and me to the hospital, and when we saw David, Shawn ran to his bed, but David was too weak to hug him. I kissed him and he smiled, but in a matter of minutes he was screaming in pain. A nurse who arrived to give David some medicine turned to me and said, "Your husband talks about you all the time, saying how much he loves you." I thanked her and said, "And I love him as much as he loves me."

As I looked around David's room, I saw lots of pictures of the three of us, but I still hadn't been told what was wrong with him. After a while, two doctors appeared in his room and finally told me: David had bladder cancer. I was completely shocked. They then said there was nothing that could be done for him and that I should take him home or to a hospice. I was holding David's hand, and I'm sure he could feel it turn to ice. I could only think that this was a bad dream, yet another living nightmare. David, my love, the father of my son, was going to die? I said to God, please, no! I was crying, pleading to the doctors: I will give you anything, everything, to make him well. They said they were very sorry, but that they had done all it was possible to do. As they left, I turned to David and said, "Darling, please tell me you won't give up like you told me before. What will I do without you?"

Lying in bed, looking sad and weak, David said, "Christine, I will always love you, and I will always be with you" and told me how he had known since summer that something was wrong. With tears in his eyes, he said, "My darling, remember everything I said. Shawn needs you. You are strong, and I want you to be strong for him. And I want you to make a new life for yourself but to keep me in your heart."

I was going crazy with grief and anger. I didn't want to leave him alone, so I spent every day and night in his room. It wasn't long before the doctors said the only way to keep him alive was to put him on a respirator and asked us if that was what we wanted. In my distraught condition, that was a question I could not answer, but David answered it for us when he said he did not want to be kept alive that way, that he did not want any more pain. I hated to expose Shawn to the sadness of his father's agonizing death, to the tears and the grief, but there was no avoiding some of it if I wanted to give them both a chance to say good-bye. One time, toward the end, when David had lost all his memory, Shawn was in his room. David kept looking at his son and said, as if surprised, "This boy looks just like me."

I said, "Yes, he does look like you," and then David gave Shawn a hug and said he loved him and he would always love him. Shawn said, "I love you, too, Daddy." I didn't cry because I didn't want Shawn to see me upset yet again, but it was hard.

The next day, I took David to a hospice. It was beyond painful to watch the man I loved more than life itself dying. David, speaking in the faint whisper that was all he could summon, thanked me for giving him the best years of his life. Shawn had spent that day with Mark, but I wanted us to be together that night, so I made a bed on a couch in David's room for him. When it was time to turn out the lights, I tucked Shawn in and then got into bed with David. I wanted him to feel he wasn't alone. We didn't know that it would be our last night together. Lying there, I talked to him constantly and would ask if he could hear me, but he didn't move or say anything. The next morning, at nine-fifteen, David passed away. I cried more than I had ever cried. I felt my life was over. I wanted to be strong for Shawn, but I couldn't help myself and started screaming Why me? Why did I live when everyone was dying around me? It was Dec. , 2008, the day I lost the most important person in my life. I looked at Shawn, who at the age of four had just lost his father, and knew my tears were more for him, even, than for me.

I decided not to take Shawn to the funeral, and, as I sat at the service, I realized I didn't know any of the people there except for David's family or understand very much of was being said, David and I having communicated in French during our years together. I felt all alone, just the way I had felt my whole life before meeting David. I was sitting near the casket, unable to stop crying, as Wald said moving things about his son and Shawn and me. I had a red rose, and at the end of the service, I walked to the casket and placed it and one of David's favorite pictures of the three of us beside him. I leaned over and kissed him, told him I loved him and left to a life I had no assurance I could manage.

17

MY LIFE AS A WIDOW AND
A SINGLE MOTHER

I decided to stay in St. Louis after David's death, and Shawn and I temporarily moved in with his cousins Joseph and Sandra Weiss and their family. They were wonderful to us, not only giving us a place to stay, but befriending us and helping me with my English. They demonstrated the true meaning of family and friendship, and without them I don't know what Shawn and I would have done. It was as stark a contrast between my earlier life and my new one as could possibly be imagined, as everyone in David's family wanted the absolute best for Shawn and me.

Unbeknownst to me, David had been diagnosed with his cancer in October 2008, with his doctors saying the disease was connected in some way to his assignment in Iraq. He returned to the States at that time, revealing to me later that he had decided not to tell me about his illness because he didn't want Shawn and me to watch him die. I had wanted to be by his side, so his decision was hard to understand, as was his family's decision to respect his wish for secrecy, but I later came to realize that the decision was another example of how David and his family expressed their love for Shawn and me.

In the days after David died, Shawn would ask if his father was "coming back," or if he could "call Dad." I would tell him, No, Shawn, Dad is busy in heaven. But Shawn was not even four years old yet, so he didn't know what that meant. Then he would say, Mom, can you ask Dad to come home? I want him to bring me a present for Christmas. It was heartbreaking to have to tell Shawn that his father wasn't coming home and wouldn't be bringing any presents. And because of the date of David's death, his funeral was the night before Christmas, so for Shawn and me it was the loneliest and saddest Christmas imaginable.

Shawn called me to his room the night after the funeral—Christmas night—and said, "Mom, I saw Dad today. He waved at me, and he told me he loved you and me. But he didn't bring me any presents. Did he forget?" I grabbed my baby and gave him a hug, but I was also crying. Shawn said, "Mama, please don't cry." Then he gave me a hug and said, "Mom, are you crying because of Dad?" I said yes, but I wanted to protect him. I didn't want him to know that his father was gone and not coming back. I climbed into bed with him and told him that Dad loved him very much and he would always be in his heart, and then I hugged him, and we fell asleep together.

During those excruciating days, I turned to God more than ever. I told him that I loved him, but I also asked why he was making me go through so much more pain after all he had put me through before. And now he was hurting another person, a son who needed his father. What had I done wrong? Why, I asked God, are you not there to stop my suffering? Losing my husband at 29, a fatherless boy, a widow with a young son, alone in a strange country. *Why?*

Yet again in my life, I was forced to start over. Having decided to stay in the U.S. to give Shawn a connection to his American family, I found a house, which, even though it was in a low-income neighborhood, was mine. The house was "old"—45 years old; older than me!—and as Shawn and I had nothing, we slept on the floor. I didn't even know where to go shopping, and it took seemingly forever to get all the paperwork done to resolve our immigration issues, to get various permits, even to get a driver's license. It wasn't helpful that I didn't speak English very well. There I was, alone with a child, in a strange city and country, my husband gone, unable to speak English, in a new neighborhood and an empty house and grieving for my lost love. I was angry and sad, but I tried my best to keep going, mainly for Shawn. I told myself I would work as hard as I could to overcome my near-paralyzing grief and to be strong for him. I knew there was no option if he were to have a chance at happiness and a normal life. One day, soon after that conversation with myself, I took Shawn to a nearby park, where we petted the animals and walked and played. Shawn caught a fish, and as I watched him enjoying himself, I found myself smiling for the first time in what seemed like forever.

As I was helping Shawn with his fish, I started talking to a beautiful woman standing nearby with her two children, a girl and her younger sibling, a boy about Shawn's age named Tyler. The three children started playing together, and the woman, whose name was Sharon, and I began talking. I learned that she had just lost her mother, so we had our grieving in common and to help each other with. Sharon was also a good Christian with a strong belief in God, so that was another connection we had. She didn't even care about my bad English or strong accent! She and her children and Shawn and I ended up becoming good friends. She was someone I could depend on for support and understanding, just as she could me. Having her in my life, having someone almost like a sister, someone who believed in God as strongly as I did, couldn't have come at a better time because it helped alleviate the loneliness that was so painful and at times disabling. Sharon brought stability and hope to my life when I needed them badly. I am happy to say that she and Tyler became and remain Shawn's and my best friends.

Two years went by, and in all that time, I made only a few other friends and never had so much as a single date or felt the need to have a boyfriend, in part because I felt that if I did, it would be a form of cheating on David. The truth was more complicated: I was scared of the real world, scared to face the reality of life. After all, I told myself, I had never dated anyone before David; all I knew was this man I had been with since the age of 19. My husband was my first boyfriend, and my first boyfriend was my husband. Growing up as I did, I never had time to be a real teenager, so I didn't know where to start with dating. And I didn't know if it was fair to Shawn to bring someone new into his life.

In other ways, though, things were getting better. I had received my residency papers (and now had a car and a driver's license), had joined a church I liked and, thinking that I was too young to sit around feeling sorry for myself, had joined a grief-therapy group. At first, I would sit quietly while the other members of the group, which met twice a week, would talk about their problems, thinking that my problems were so different from theirs that they wouldn't be interested and, in any case, not wanting to talk about them under any circumstances. I was used to keeping things in my heart and close. Besides, I said, even if I tell people about my problems, they will not care because they have problems of their own. I soon found out I was wrong.

After letting me remain silent for several meetings, the woman who had organized the group asked me one day how I felt and if I had anything to say. When I hesitated, she said the only way I would be able to move on would be to talk about it, adding that it was OK if I didn't feel ready and that everyone was glad I was there regardless. Then a sad young woman told about her husband who had been killed after just a few months of marriage. She was crying, so I went to her and gave her a hug. As I couldn't find anything to say to her to make her feel better, I started talking about my life—the genocide, all the people I had lost—most of all David and Chantal—about my terrible childhood, about Shawn and about how glad I was to be alive with a son I loved. One of the women in the group came over to me and said, "Christine, you've just made our problems go away."

After hearing this and telling the group the story of my life, I felt better: my pain lifted, and I felt a rush of positive feelings, as if in talking about my I could allow myself to feel more wholly human. Sorrow's black wing was no longer draped across my brow, even if only for a moment.

I was aware that in talking about the abuse I suffered at the hands of my father, I was describing a part of my life that I'd never shared with anyone, except Chantal. For all that David loved me, comforted me and made me feel empowered, and for how natural he made it feel for me to delve into the horrors I had seen and lived through once I felt ready to talk about them, I could never bring myself to tell him about the abuse. Maybe I was still too scarred. Or maybe I wanted to spare him.

Following the meeting with the group, I went home and took a hot shower and decided to visit David's grave. As I drove to the cemetery, with my Bible and David's picture on the seat beside me, I started crying and talking to him and looking at his picture. I wasn't paying attention to how fast I was driving when a police car came up behind me with its lights on. I stopped, and the officer walked up and greeted me politely. Seeing that I had been crying, he asked if I were OK and then asked why I had been speeding. I told him I was in a hurry to get to my husband's grave. The officer didn't give me a ticket; instead, he said, "I'm sorry," asked if I were OK to drive and, when I said yes, said he would follow me for a while to make sure I got to the cemetery safely. It was as though David had sent someone to look over me.

I spent several hours at David's grave, talking to him and reading my Bible. Crying, I asked David to remember his promise to protect Shawn and me and asked God to take care of him and to give him the best place in Heaven. After I finished praying, it started to rain. I got up to go home but then changed my mind and returned to the gravesite, wanting to stay longer. It began to rain harder, but I didn't care. After two hours in the rain, I finally got in my car and went home, talking and crying like a crazy person in my sorrow without end.

When I got home, I showered and took a nap, something I never did. I started dreaming and in my dream I saw David, who was telling me how much he loved me but that it was time for me to move on. "I want you to be happy," he said. "I don't want you to be alone and sad. You are a strong woman. I know you can do it." I woke up and, of course, David wasn't there. But for a minute, because my dream was so vivid, I'd thought I would find him beside me. After I got up, I decided that now was the time for me to try to start my life anew. Having called Mark and made plans for Shawn to spend the night, I went to my closet and found a nice dress. Then I called some friends and asked them if they wanted to go out. One of them, Becky, was surprised. "Are you sure?" she said. "Are you OK? We've being begging you to go out forever. This is so exciting!"

I'd always been thin, but now, after all the stress, pain, sadness and borderline malnutrition during David's illness and death, I was downright emaciated. Nevertheless, I found a dress that flattered me and met my friends for my "coming out" night. We went to a restaurant and then to a nightclub, where almost everybody was drinking or drunk. My friends tried to get me to drink, to "have fun," but I said no because I was afraid that if I resorted to alcohol just once to help me forget my problems, I would want to drink all the time. I told them that even though I had lots of problems and had lived through more pain than humanly possible, I would work through it using my strength and the love of my son and God. At first, everyone teased me, but then, seeing my earnestness, they said, "Good for you."

Even though I was glad to have "come out" with my friends that night, it confirmed one thing more than ever: My only thoughts were about David and our 10 wonderful years together. I couldn't think of anything, or anyone, other than that.

I know that I will always be viewed as a widow with a child in an "adopted" country and a survivor of genocide. That is how I will be characterized by others, and I've come to accept that.

Shawn is my angel. He is a smart, caring young man who is growing beautifully, and who, at nine, looks just like his father. Whenever I'm feeling down, Shawn comes to me and hugs me, and every time he looks at me and smiles and tells me he loves me he makes all my problems go away. Thanks to Shawn, and to God for bringing him into my life, I have been able to put my past behind me and am happier than I have ever been, although when I say put the past behind me, I don't mean that I've managed to forget it, just that I've managed to live with it.

The only thing I care about is that Shawn has a mother who loves him and will do anything for him, do all the things my parents never did for me, and who will be there for him twenty-four hours a day. I tell him that I love him all the time because I know that makes him feel safe and wanted. Once Shawn asked me if I had any pictures of my birthday parties as a child, and I had to tell him that I never had a birthday party. That made him sad for me, so he promised that he would make cupcakes and draw a card for me on my birthday. And that is just what he did! Today on my birthday, I don't do anything for myself. Instead, I remember my childhood, think about children who may be going through the same things I went through and feel that if I could I would save all those suffering from abuse by their parents. Every year on my birthday that is all I wish for.

Actually, I have been saving children, in a small way. I contribute to the support of a group of Rwandan orphans who live with Valentine in Kigali. I am proud that the children all go to school and that four of them are even getting their medical degrees. It's satisfying knowing I'm helping others who are struggling in some of the ways I did and giving them the hope I never had.

No matter how hard I try to keep it away, to "put it behind me," the past haunts me always, often in unanticipated ways. I recently became friendly with a woman named Ratifa, a survivor of the genocide in her own country, Burundi, whose president, Cyprian Ntayamira, died in the same plane crash that killed President Habyarimana. One day Ratifa and I were having coffee when she started crying. She proceeded to tell me how she had lost her husband and children in Burundi's genocide, and how her mother's house was burned down while she and Ratifa's father were inside. She said there was nothing left for her, and how lonely she was in the U.S. She told me how hard it was for her to survive during the genocide, and as she sat there, sad and wiping her tears, I didn't say anything about my own trials, giving Ratifa the respect of listening to her story. I said to her she should take life one day at a time, not give up and try, no matter how hard, to find something positive to live for. I also told her how important faith can be in restoring a degree of hope and peace to one's life.

Ratifa looked at me and said that I was a strong woman. When I asked her why she said that, she said she could see it in my eyes. I told her that I had suffered way too much in my sad life, but I was still fighting and I didn't plan to give up, especially because of Shawn. Later, when, at Ratifa's request, I shared with her some of the darkness that had been my life, she broke down in tears, this time for me, and said that she couldn't grasp how my parents could treat their children like that, that her parents had loved and protected her and her brother and had literally given their lives in that burning house to save them.

The question of forgiveness is one I wrestle with, still, after all this time. One Sunday in church the lesson was on the topic of forgiving, the point being that no matter what, it is always good to forgive, that we should look no further than God and the way he forgives us. After the service, I went up to the pastor to ask him some questions. "Would you be able to forgive someone who killed your family and friends?" I said. "Would you be able to forgive someone who destroyed your childhood?"

The pastor looked at me and said, "Yes, I would. I know it wouldn't be easy, but I would."

When I told him I was a Rwandan survivor, he became very sad and said now he understood my questions. Then the two of us prayed together, and afterward he said, "Marie-Christine, I know you are a strong woman. I know you can get beyond all this. You are here by the grace of God." I thanked him for praying with me and for his wise counsel.

One of the biggest changes in my life is that Valentine and I have become close. We talk all the time, and I don't blame her anymore for what she did. I help support her orphanage, and I am learning to love her and move forward, looking toward the future. With my father, however, it was a lot harder.

Born into poverty but, equipped with a college degree and a willingness to work hard, a man who became moderately prosperous, he lost everything in the genocide and had to start completely over. Unfortunately, he later made some bad business decisions and once again lost everything, including his homes and his cars, so I let him stay in my home. But in my heart, I still reviled him, and David and others would ask why I was helping him when he had mistreated me so. I didn't have an answer. All I know is that whenever people ask me to help them, I say yes. Whenever my stepbrother Placide, who is in medical school in Romania, asks me for money, I give it to him. I've always been that way, and I always will be. Maybe it's one way I deal with the pain, or maybe the guilt, of being a survivor. What's even more surprising to me and my friends is that I keep helping even when people don't acknowledge my help or say thank you or behave badly toward me. But that doesn't stop me, nor will it.

In 2013, Valentine called me, saying that my father was very ill and was in the hospital with pain in his head. A few days later, she said the doctors told him he had cancer and needed brain surgery as quickly as possible. I talked to my father, who said, "My daughter, I am so sorry that I wasn't a good father. I am so sorry for all the pain I caused you. I am sorry for destroying your life, and I would ask you to please forgive me, and if you can't forgive me I will not have my surgery. I deserve to suffer, too." He started crying, and he said, "I know I will die." I told him that I had forgiven him a long time ago and that that was in the past; now it was time to focus on the here and now. "Dad," I said, "you need the operation."

He said OK, but that if I were not there, he wouldn't do it. "I want you to be here, in case I die," he said.

"I want to see you first." I told him to have the operation and not to wait, that I would be there as soon as I could. While we were talking, he continued to apologize, and I told him if he really meant what he said he should have the operation, which he said he would do.

I decided to take Shawn with me to Rwanda, and we arrived at Valentine's and my father's house, where he had been sent to rest up before going back to the hospital for the operation. In his state of dementia, he didn't recognize me or Shawn. As he wept for the pain he had caused me, I told him again that I had forgiven him long ago, even though it wasn't exactly true, and that seemed to make him feel better, which had been my intention.

I tried to do everything I could to make him feel better; not only did I tell him I had forgiven him, I stayed with him, I prayed for him, and I paid his hospital bills. During my visit, I saw my friend Nathalie, and we spent a lot of time together. She couldn't understand how I could be so accommodating to my father after the way he had treated me. I said that under the circumstances it was time to give him another chance and that my decision to return was for him, to offer my support. I told Nathalie I'd come to realize forgiving makes us stronger and feel better because we are making others feel better, and that that was why I was trying to forgive. Even though I could tell Nathalie didn't agree with me, she hugged me and told me how proud she was of me and how much she respected me for being so kind to those who had done such evil.

My father's operation was declared a success, and he returned home with a reprieve of his death sentence. One day, toward the end of Shawn's and my visit, everyone was in the living room when my father started crying like a child for no apparent reason. No one did or said anything to make him feel better, so I walked over and said, "Dad, I love you." It was the first time I'd ever said that to him or to anyone in my family other than Chantal, but the most amazing thing was that I actually meant it. It truly came from my heart. Later, as I lay in my room, I was astonished at how relieved and free I felt, as if I had untethered myself and now could fly.

Everyone knew that my father didn't have much longer to live. I wanted to be by his side at the end; however, I didn't want Shawn to have to go through another wrenching death as he had with his father, so I decided we would leave and return home. A few days after we got back, Valentine called with the news that my father had died. I listened with little emotion, whether it was because I had never truly forgiven—and certainly never forgotten—what he did or because my heart had grown numb from all the pain, I didn't, and don't, know. All I knew was that I could finally put an unspeakable part of my life behind me.

The war in Rwanda and my terrible childhood left me with marks and scars in my heart forever. So even though I live in America, in a nice suburb with a nice house and nice possessions, I am still that Rwandan girl who grew up poor and abused and molested, then somehow survived a genocide, who struggles still with her past. I fear that that is how it will always be, and my only hope is that it will not prevent me from being the best mother I can be to my wonderful son. I have truly forgiven Valentine, and we now, improbably, have a loving and wonderful relationship. I say "improbably," but it was because I was able, with God's help, to absolve her and give her a chance. I see her as a loving and wonderful person who makes me very happy and with whom I focus on the future, not only with Shawn, but with the orphans we both help.

As I write this book, I am gratified to say that my life continues to get better. Shawn is growing and happy, I like living in Missouri, and I have good friends and deep relationships. I like who I am. I have found that sharing my past in this way has helped heal my heart, and I hope it will help others to heal theirs and remember never to give up, no matter how dire the situation may appear. I didn't, and I am the better for it. When people ask me how I managed to outlast everything in my life, I tell them it was due to my determination and the grace of God. I tell them, pray with an open heart and God will help you, just as he did me. True, I will always be that poor girl from Rwanda. But I will also always be that strong woman who survived.

AFTERWORD

My beloved grandmother Leontina, the most important person in my life, died on Oct. 19, 1999, following a long struggle with cancer. She was 76.

David, my incomparable husband, was born in Algeria, the son of American missionaries Ward R. and Raverda Williams, wonderful parents to their three children. Ward, who lived to 96, died in 2009. Raverda, who was healthy till her final days, died in 2000 in her sleep. Sadly, she passed away before Shawn was born, so she and her grandson never had a chance to share each other's love.

My mother and I talk every once in a while, and I try to keep her in my and Shawn's life, but it is difficult because we live so far apart. She still resides in Romania.

In 2004, PBS broadcast "Ghosts of Rwanda," about the genocide. To view the documentary and the" Frontline" web page "The Triumph of Evil," visit my website at humandarkside.com.

CPSIA information can be obtained at www.ICGtesting.com
Printed in the USA
LVOW08*2314270516

490321LV00002B/4/P